LET THEM EAT

Cupcakes

DEDICATION

To all the cakers and bakers out there who find joy in measure, color, taste, and composition. To the sweet tooths, to the crumb lovers, to whoever invented GLITTER CHERRIES, to sprinkles, to BUTTER. To my TRIBE, to my DEREK—my rock, my mentor, my most cherished. To Marie Anne and her flour shop for guiding me here. To those who are KIND, those who CREATE, those who EAT CAKE, and those who CELEBRATE. To all my BIG FISH. And to my future little fish—to me, to us, to all of you.

LET THEM EAT
Cupcakes

100 CUPCAKE RECIPES TO RULE THEM ALL

GABRIELLE COTE

CIDER MILL PRESS

BOOK PUBLISHERS

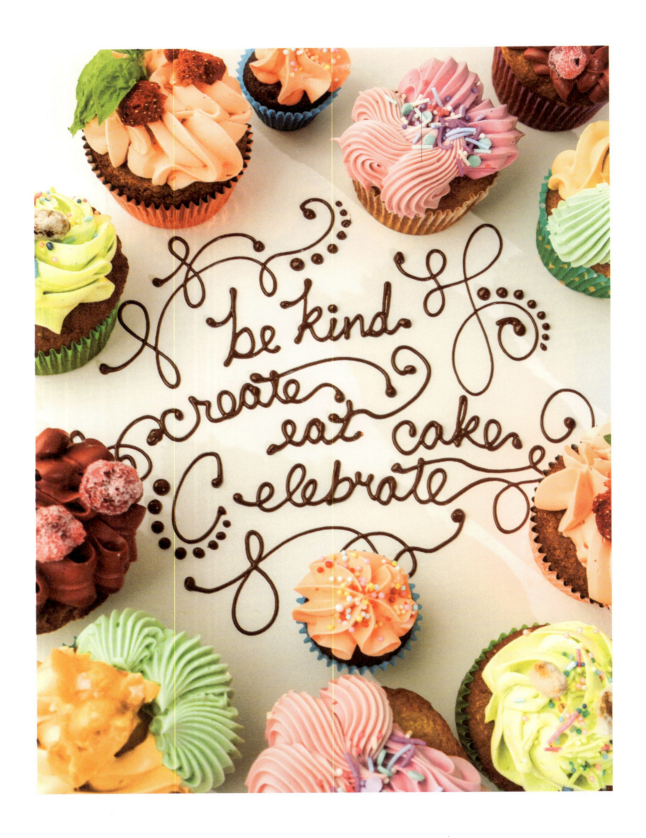

be kind
create
eat cake
celebrate

Contents

INTRODUCTION

I used to think I just drifted into baking. But now I feel like baking chose me, alerting me to the connections that can be made through food.

After all, haven't you ever heard that the way to someone's heart is a fresh baked ... anything?

If you have this book in your hands, the thought of making tiny, dazzling cakes has no doubt been on your mind. You've wondered: Can I do this? Do I have time? The tools? Where do I start?

Start here. Master the basics, figure out who are with a piping bag in your hand. Make a mess, then make an even bigger mess. Mismeasure, remeasure, burn things. Time yourself, be yourself. Never stop learning. Ask questions, research, and taste all of the things.

By keeping this and the guidance provided in this book in mind, one can master the basics, and start thinking like a chef.

A pastry chef, actually.

That job is a little bit different than the conventional understanding of what a chef does. A pastry chef is charged with taking particular flavors and finding ways to express and articulate them. It's not like a piece of steak, where the flavor depends on the quality of the meat and the cooking method—a cupcake is made from scratch. Learn how your ingredients work and then learn how to manipulate them. Don't overthink it—a baker confident enough to keep things simple is a successful baker.

That's how I started. And at first, I didn't find cake all that easy. Which was OK, since my career took me far beyond the basics—I found myself quickly pushing the boundaries of pastry, and eventually, I turned salty (I worked on the savory side of things, serving as Sous Chef at the prestigious White Barn Inn in Kennebunkport).

I did find my way back to pastry, though, leaving behind the madness of the restaurant world for the madness of my own—opening my own business, Big Fish Cake Studio.

I went along happily for a few months, until someone at a bridal shower asked: "How's your cupcake business doing?"

I was annoyed. I thought I was so much better than cupcakes. I thought they were for less talented, less ambitious artisans than myself.

Is that what people think I'm doing with my life? I huffed inwardly. *Cupcakes?*

What I failed to see then, and understand now, is that cupcakes are art. Yes, they are adorable, tasty, and eye-catching. But they are also incredibly dramatic, expressive, and evocative. I missed this when I was starting my business because I was convinced that, in order to justify my creations, everything had to operate at the highest-possible level. Just like I did when I started in kitchens, just like I did when I first started baking.

Fortunately, I got over that quickly. Cupcakes are humbling, and they are also rewarding. Incredibly so. I soon realized that they are a symbol of nurturing, of celebration, of community. They are versatile, they are unique, and they have the potential to take whatever shape you want them to.

As there are no rules to cupcakes beyond the fundamentals tied to all baked goods, they provide a perfect opportunity for you to express yourself, and will help you discover who you are as a baker. Cupcakes are now my favorite thing to bake, and I regret all the cupcake orders I turned down at the beginning of my business endeavors. They are fun, and they are fundamental.

In many ways, my career is just the typical version of a chef's life—climb the ladder, find the best kitchens, learn all you can, sacrifice a lot in order to succeed. Working in restaurants was hard, and demanding, but, after 12 years, it was a world I knew, a world I believed I had carved myself a space in.

Then that world got turned upside down by the pandemic. I thought it might pass in six months or so, but, as we all know, it arrived, and it did not leave.

We quarantined.

I lost my job. My big girl chef job.

Following a moment of panic, I started problem solving, and found some hope.

The year before the pandemic, I lost two of my biggest mentors. When I lost my job, it felt like the world was closing in on me, and fast.

But, as we all know, tough times can foster strength, and I found myself with more motivation than ever, determined not to let my abilities be pushed aside, and to make those that I'd lost proud.

I knew that owning my own business it would be the best route back to my pastry roots. I also knew I was done managing people for a while. Everything else was up for grabs.

As always, I found most of the answers I needed while painting. Art has always been my meditative space, a gift I owe to my incredibly artistic mother. For me, painting was purely a means of expression and release—I never really considered making a life out of it, but I did discover, somewhere along the way, that I am most in tune with myself when I take the time to paint.

One day during that fraught time, while working with acrylics and palette knives, and wearing, as always, an old chef's coat as a smock, I realized the paint was just like buttercream. Altering paint is just a matter of ratios, as is buttercream. And, since I often manipulate the body of my paints to get different results, I realized I could do that with buttercream as well.

A simple equation came into my head, Buttercream + Ability = Gabby's New Path.

I figured that, in spite of the pandemic, people will still get married and have weddings. People will continue to have birthdays and celebrate them at parties with close friends and family.

Sure, I thought, I'll spend all of my money building myself a kitchen, and I'll be fine. After all, I figured, people still needed cake.

And though the pandemic continued to do its best to keep us apart, in the end, I was right.

I decided to name this venture Big Fish Cake Studio, after the mentors that I lost. And though I know they would have warned me that heading out on my own was a massive risk, the truth is that they'd put me in a position where I was able to handle that risk. Still, I didn't realize how much they had taught me until I started down this path by myself.

Now they feel close and I feel far less afraid—give me a few days to bake and build cakes or cupcakes for a big event and I am in heaven. Cake is my canvas, and I feel at ease—at least when I'm not in the weeds, which does, inevitably, still happen.

Though I definitely do not have a well-oiled machine just yet, at the time of I'm gearing up for my fourth wedding season. Considering where I started out, that feels like more than a small indication that things are headed in the right direction.

None of this would have been possible without Derek, my partner in life, and my partner in business. Our story is a little wild, moving from acquaintances to teammates and then to enemies. It took years for mutual respect to blossom between us, never mind love. Eventually, he took a chance on me and our friendship blossomed. During the next few years, he taught me most of what I know about working in a kitchen, and we started making a difference while working together. Eventually, we started looking at each other funny, and fell in love.

Derek also found who he was through food, first as a chef, and then as a kickass photographer of all things food and beverage. He has become just as acclaimed working behind the lens as he was following 20+ years working in restaurants all over the world. In short, he's a force of nature.

Today, we run our businesses right alongside each other, in the creative space we built, Studio 242. It has a cozy client space for consultations, a full commercial kitchen, a suite that is primarily used for cake building (though any chef could come in and work there), a full photo studio equipped with all of Derek's toys, and more. We spend our days collaborating, working on our crafts, blasting tunes, and eating lots of cake scraps.

To give you some idea of how we work: when the opportunity to author this book arrived, I was expecting to hire Derek as the photographer. But as he was at work on a cookbook of his own (his seventh!), in addition to all of his other gigs, he did not have time to shoot mine. Instead, he handed me a camera, built me a backdrop to style my cupcakes against, and gave me a crash course in the basics.

He was in charge of handling files and editing—but man did I gain a whole lot more respect for the guy during this process. To be frank, this book kicked my ass. I am not passionate about photography, but it has helped me see everything I create in a new light, and it was nice to once again follow in Derek's footsteps. Now, I often assist him on larger sets as his "sous," just because we just dance so well together when we work. We speak the same language and know how to support each other.

The day-to-day of a small business owner isn't easy—it's a lifestyle, not a living. There's so much freedom, but then, at the same time, so little. Every day is different, every season brings new challenges and features new goals. The endless can't-miss deadlines, the piling expenses. But at the end of the day, I get to bake and decorate cakes, and do it beside the love of my life, who is pursuing his own passion. We are making our way as food artists and we get to do that right next to each other—life is sweet.

I hope this book helps some baker out there make their own way, and realize their dreams. I hope it can alleviate some of the needless trepidation that keeps so many people from baking.

Really, I just hope it brings people joy, and encourages them to find space for a little more cake in their lives.

ESSENTIAL TECHNIQUES & TOOLS

*A*s baking well is based on one's ability to master the fundamentals, I want to take a moment and go in-depth into everything from measuring and mixing to working with your home oven. Small things make a big difference in the kitchen, and often determine whether the result is a success or a disappointment.

Do yourself a huge favor and set up your kitchen the night before you plan to bake. The morning of, scale your ingredients too. This will make the process of scaling and mixing much easier, since doing both at the same time takes a lot of practice. Proper measuring is the most important piece of a finished baked good—make sure you are not rushing or stressed during this part of the process. If you have everything set up beforehand, you can take your time, focus, and learn.

Make sure your equipment is clean, clean, CLEAN before you start mixing. I mean spotless. Any residual fat or grease left on the mixing bowl, mixer attachments, whisk, or spatula can completely keep the proteins from incorporating air during the early stages of the mixing process. This means you'll have a denser, less voluminous finished baked good. Also, I wash all of my stainless steel pieces by hand. The mixers and attachments have an exterior coating that does not stand up to dishwasher temperatures and eventually will come off. If that happens, then you'll be introducing different pH levels to your eggs, which will affect their ability to foam.

Learn to use metric measurements when baking, as it will save you time, prevent waste, and result in less dishes, since you can just add everything to the same mixing bowl.

Sifting your dry ingredients is important for getting the airy, moist result you want. To do this, I combine all of the dry ingredients in a bowl and then I sift the mixture through a fine-mesh tamis over a piece of parchment paper. Then I fold the parchment paper lengthwise and gently shake it over the mixing bowl—this makes it easy to incorporate the dry ingredients into the batter in increments.

Pay attention, clean as you go, and don't be too hard on yourself.

MIXING

When it comes to mixing a cake batter, there are a few approaches, all of which will produce different moisture levels and crumb structure. Some are straightforward, some are difficult. Again, baking is built off fundamentals, and these methods will carry you through all of the recipes in this book. Once you master them, you will be much more confident, and have way more time to focus on the decorating and design aspects of your art.

CREAMING METHOD

This is the most common mixing method, known to achieve a sturdy yet soft texture.

◇ **Start with room-temperature ingredients:** It's crucial to have softened butter at room temperature. This makes it easier to cream the butter with sugar and trap air in the mixture, which will result in a batter that has a lighter texture.

◇ **Combine the butter and sugar:** Place the softened butter and sugar in the work bowl of a stand mixer fitted with the paddle attachment (you can also use a hand mixer or a sturdy spatula) and beat until the mixture is light and fluffy. My key when using the creaming method is remembering not to rush this part of the process, and I advise you to adapt it as well.

◇ **Add the eggs (if they are in the recipe):** Once the butter and sugar have been creamed, the eggs are often added one at a time, beating well after each addition. This patient incorporating of the eggs ensures that they are evenly distributed and contributes to the structure of the final product.

◇ **Incorporate the remaining ingredients:** After the butter, sugar, and eggs have been combined, the recipe typically calls for incorporating the dry ingredients such as flour, baking powder, salt, etc. These are usually added in stages, alternating with liquids like milk or buttermilk, to ensure that the batter is even without overmixing. When alternating between adding the dry and wet ingredients, I like to use this technique—one-third dry, half liquid, one-third dry, half liquid, and finish with the remaining one-third of the dry ingredients. Make sure to remember to scrape down the work bowl between these additions to prevent clumping and avoid overmixing.

◇ **Mix until just combined:** It's essential not to overmix the batter once the dry ingredients are added. Overmixing can lead to a tough or dense texture in the final baked goods.

STRAIGHT METHOD

Also known as the blended method, this is the most convenient and straightforward of the basic mixing methods. All you need is a bowl and a whisk! It's especially useful when you want to minimize cleanup and simplify the baking process without sacrificing the quality of the final product. Recipes using the straight method tend to be super moist, and usually consist of liquid fats and a higher ratio of sugar to flour.

◇ **Combine dry ingredients:** In a mixing bowl, combine all the dry ingredients such as flour, sugar, salt, baking powder, and any spices or leavening agents called for in the recipe.

◇ **Add the wet ingredients:** Make a well in the center of the dry ingredients. Pour the liquid ingredients (like eggs, milk, oil, melted butter, flavor extracts) into the well.

◇ **Mix until just combined:** Using a whisk, a wooden spoon, or a mixer on low speed, gently mix the wet and dry ingredients together until just combined. It's crucial not to overmix; a few lumps in the batter are acceptable.

◇ **Fold in additional ingredients:** If the recipe includes additional ingredients like nuts, chocolate chips, dried fruits, or other mix-ins, fold them into the batter gently until evenly distributed.

SPONGE METHOD

The sponge method, also known as the foaming method, is used to create light and airy cakes, such as genoise, chiffon, and sponge cakes. The sponge method is ideal for cakes where a light and fluffy texture is desired. When using this method, it's important to handle the batter gently to preserve the aeration achieved during the initial mixing of eggs and sugar. The resulting batter will be super-smooth so do not be thrown off by its thinner consistency—it will rise in the oven, and be moist and tender.

◇ **Prepare the base (sponge):** Whisk or beat the egg component (eggs or egg yolks, depending on the recipe) with the sugar until the mixture becomes thick, pale, and foamy. This step incorporates air into the batter, which will help leaven the cupcakes.

◇ **Add flavorings:** Once the eggs and sugar are well beaten and have increased in volume, add flavorings such as vanilla extract or citrus zest.

◇ **Fold in dry ingredients:** Add the dry ingredients (flour, baking powder, baking soda, salt, etc.) to the foamy egg mixture in small batches and use a gentle folding motion with a rubber spatula to incorporate the dry ingredients. The goal is to thoroughly incorporate the dry ingredients without deflating the air bubbles created during the initial beating.

◇ **Incorporate fats:** If the recipe includes fats like melted butter or oil, add them last and fold to incorporate them into the batter.

◇ **Bake immediately:** Once the batter is mixed via the sponge method, it's important to bake it immediately. The air bubbles trapped in the batter will help the cake rise during baking, resulting in cupcakes with a light and airy texture.

GLUTEN-FREE METHOD

Creating gluten-free cakes involves some adjustments to traditional baking methods, due to the absence of gluten, which provides structure and elasticity in cupcakes made via traditional methods. By following these steps and using high-quality gluten-free ingredients, you can create delicious gluten-free cakes with a tender and moist crumb. That said: gluten-free baking is tricky, and I highly encourage you to practice on your own before baking for others.

◇ **Select gluten-free flour:** Start by choosing either a gluten-free flour blend or a specific gluten-free flour like rice flour, almond flour, or coconut flour. Ensure the flour is labeled as gluten-free to avoid any cross contamination. I used to make my own flour blends, but it is very challenging, especially for beginner bakers. I highly recommend King Arthur's Gluten-Free Measure for Measure Flour. It is a convenient, 1:1 substitute for all-purpose or cake flours and works with most recipes found in this book.

◇ **Blend dry ingredients:** In a mixing bowl, whisk together the gluten-free flour, baking powder or baking soda, salt, and any other dry ingredients specified in your recipe. This ensures even distribution of leavening agents and flavor throughout the cake.

◇ **Cream fats and sugars:** In a separate bowl, cream together the fats (butter, oil, etc.) and sugars (sugar, brown sugar, or alternative sweeteners). Creaming helps incorporate air into the mixture, contributing to a lighter texture in the final cake.

◇ **Add wet ingredients:** Add the wet ingredients to the creamed mixture. This typically includes eggs (or egg substitutes for vegan options), vanilla extract, and any other liquids like milk or dairy-free alternatives.

◇ **Combine dry and wet ingredients:** Gradually add the dry ingredients to the batter, mixing until just combined. Avoid overmixing, as this can lead to a dense, gummy, or tough texture in gluten-free cakes.

◇ **Bake immediately:** The power of leavening agents is time sensitive to begin with, and they need to work a little bit harder in gluten-free batters. Be sure to pop these cakes right in the oven after mixing.

◇ **Baking time and temperature:** Gluten-free cupcakes may require slightly different baking times than traditional cupcakes. I always add a minimum of 6 minutes to baking times for gluten-free cupcakes, since they are hard to overbake, and if slightly undercooked, even at 200°F, they may have that undesirable flour taste. I also cook gluten-free cupcakes in a slightly warmer oven.

USING A PIPING BAG

I can't express how much of a difference using a piping bag makes when baking cupcakes. If you want a clean and organized kitchen, it's the only way to go. I always use a bain-marie to hold my piping bags, folding the top half of the piping bag over the rim of the container.

Once the piping bag is ready, simply pour the batter into it, using a rubber spatula to get every last bit, and then twist the bag to keep it shut.

Hold the bag with your off hand, squeezing the twisted portion between your thumb and index finger. Flip the bag over so the tip is pointing up and cut off the tip. Use your other hand to pinch the opening shut. Flip the bag over and hold it over your cupcake liners. Release the tip and fill the liners until they are three-quarters full, letting gravity help you out.

For buttercreams, I follow the same exact process in terms of filling and handling the piping bag.

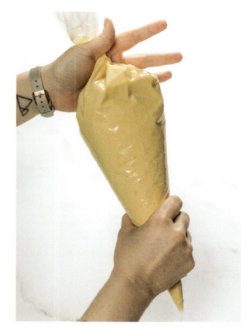

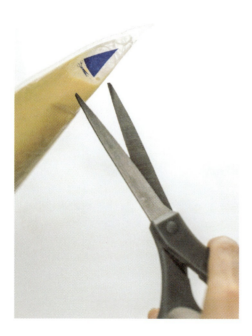

BAKING

Baking is the least forgiving phase in pastry and dessert making. But if you learn your equipment, remember that you are smarter than the doughs and batters, keep from over-thinking, and keep these fundamentals in mind, you can succeed every time.

OVEN TEMPERATURE

Every kitchen is different, and every oven is different. If your oven is less than five years old, it is likely to be hotter inside than the temperature you select. If it is older than five years, your oven may have trouble coming up to and retaining certain temperatures. I highly suggest buying an oven thermometer that you can attach to one of the racks inside your oven, as it will help you better understand your oven and find your ideal temperature for cupcake baking. For my oven, which is a large commercial convection oven, I bake all my cakes and cupcakes at 325°F. For a conventional oven, I recommend 350°F.

TIME

Baking times will vary per recipe, but cupcakes are small, and thus it is much easier to tell if they are baked or underbaked. I aim for an internal temperature of 200°F for cupcakes, and I recommend buying a digital pastry thermometer so that you can accurately determine this. Miniature cupcakes only take about 10 minutes to bake, while average-sized cupcakes take between 20 and 25 minutes. I often will set a timer for 10 minutes, then rotate my pans, and set a timer for 10 more minutes. After 20 minutes, I check the internal temperature of the cupcakes every minute or so until they are done.

MOISTURE

Cupcakes tend to have a shorter shelf life than cakes due to their tendency to dry out when exposed to air, so the more moisture you can trap, the longer the cupcakes can remain delicious. To attain the highest possible levels of moisture, I always cover my cupcakes soon after removing them from the oven. First, I let them rest in the pans for about 5 minutes. Then, using a gloved hand and an offset spatula, I transfer the cupcakes to a cupcake holder and cover them tightly so that all of the moisture is trapped inside as they cool to room temperature. Don't freak out when the cupcake liners seem wet—they will dry out!

EFFICIENCY

As soon as I put a batch of cupcakes in the oven, I take that time to clean and prepare my kitchen for decorating. First clean, then scale your buttercream. When the baked cupcakes are properly stored and cooling, start preparing the buttercream. Once the buttercream is done, the cupcakes should be cool enough to decorate. And voilà— you're working like a chef now.

THE FINISHING TOUCH

Finally, we arrive at the fun part of cupcake making! This is where you can express yourself, give your inner designer an opportunity to shine, and put the, ahem, icing on the cake.

This piece of the process is where I fell love with the craft of cake and cupcake making, and it remains my very favorite part of my job. Once you're able to keep these techniques in mind, you'll find that you can let your imagination run wild and let the proper approach reveal itself. Don't believe me? Would you be shocked if I told you I didn't design any cupcake in this book ahead of time? Each session, I would get everything set up and then just try to have fun.

Cupcakes are fairly easy to make look good, because they have the advantage of already being adorable. Trust the process, trust yourself, and take your time, and you'll end up with cupcakes that look as good as they taste.

HOW TO FILL A CUPCAKE

As cupcakes are small vessels, I suggest that you follow what I tell my clients—one filling is the maximum. When filling, I use an 804 tip to remove the centers of the cupcakes. Then I use a finer piping tip to fill the cupcakes with the jam, curd, ganache, or caramel.

MIXING COLORS

It is very easy to overthink coloring your buttercreams. But if you add colors in increments, and keep in mind that soft and pale hues are better fits for the modern aesthetic, you'll always be on the right track. To ensure that I have a cohesive look, I like to work with two to three colors per batch. Once I have my color palette in mind, I will color the first portion of buttercream, then add a bit of that color to the second portion of buttercream, which will keep them complementary. If you're looking for more contrast in a set of three colors, I would use this technique with just two portions, so you have two that are similar and one that is distinct.

PIPING

I have a large collection of piping tips, but I like to stick with medium tips for cupcake decorating. Similar to my rule of using two to three colors per batch, I like to stick to the same amount of textures. We want the cupcakes to look good, but not too busy. When piping, I try to use a couple of designs per batch. For example, in a batch of 24 cupcakes where I'm using three colors, I might do eight that use one color and one tip, eight that have two colors and two different tips, and eight with three colors and three different tips. When you're first getting the hang of this, I suggest making extra buttercream so you can practice on a piece of parchment paper before trying out your designs on the cupcakes.

WORKING WITH MULTIPLE COLORS

There will be times when you want to combine all of your colors and pipe them together. To do this, lay two pieces of plastic wrap on a work surface. Having two layers gives it more strength and will prevent the buttercream from spilling out.

Next, spoon your colors in a line on the plastic wrap. Some would pipe these lines so that they are perfectly even, but I am a bit more relaxed when it comes to decorating. Carefully roll up the plastic so that the buttercream becomes a cylinder, using a bowl scraper if needed to push any excess air out.

Squeeze and twist the ends of the plastic wrap and roll the cylinder tighter and tighter. If you're struggling to get the proper tightness during this step, moisten the work surface with a damp paper towel. This will help the plastic cylinder catch on the work surface and make tightening it and rolling it easier. Tie one end of the rolled buttercream closed and cut off the other end. Place the cylinder, cut end first, into a piping bag and squeeze the buttercream out, raising the cylinder as the buttercream comes out in order to keep it from getting all mushed together. After that, pipe away! I think rosettes are a great shape to show off the mix of colors with this technique.

MIXING SPRINKLES

I strongly suggest buying yourself a large container of white nonpareils and mixing your own sprinkles. To do this, simply place a bit of luster dust in a small container, add the nonpareils, cover the container, and shake until the sprinkles are coated. This is a great way to save money, time, and space.

STENCILING

Stenciling is a super-fun and easy way to add an impressive touch to your cupcakes. To do this, pipe a large dome of buttercream on a cupcake. I always use a large round piping tip when stenciling, but you can also just cut the tip of the piping bag and pipe, though this will not create an even dome/circle. Line a baking sheet with parchment paper, turn the cupcake upside down, and gently press it on the baking sheet until the buttercream is flat. Chill in the refrigerator for 15 minutes. Remove from the refrigerator, place the stencil over the buttercream, and gently spread buttercream over the stencil. Carefully peel the stencil away, and you're done.

EDIBLE PRINTS

I held off on getting an edible printer for years, but eventually broke down and discovered that it is a game changer, enabling me to take my decorating to a higher level. I use a program called Canva to design custom images and download stock photos. I've found that printing on frosting sheets results in the best color.

To assemble an edible plaque for my cupcakes, I use a razor blade to cut circles out of my chosen design. Next, I roll a piece of fondant out on a cornstarch-dusted cutting board until it is thin. I cut the fondant into the same-sized circles as those I just cut out of my design, brush them with some piping gel, and lay the edible images on top. I then let the plaques dry for a few hours so they do not bend or break while on top of the cupcakes.

ESSENTIAL TECHNIQUES & TOOLS   23

INGREDIENTS & EQUIPMENT

The following lists are items one will want to have on hand in order to properly prepare the recipes in this book. Some other ingredients and equipment may be required in certain instances, but for the majority of the recipes, these will put you in a great position to succeed.

WET INGREDIENTS & FATS

Eggs
Canola oil
Olive oil
Coconut oil
Milk
Heavy cream
Vanilla paste
Crisco
Sour cream
Water

DRY INGREDIENTS

All-purpose flour
Cake flour
Baking soda
Baking powder
Salt
Sugar
Brown sugar
Confectioners' sugar
Cocoa powder

BAKING EQUIPMENT

Stand mixer
Digital scale
Measuring cups and spoons
Cupcake pans/muffin tins
Digital pastry thermometer
Oven

DECORATING TOOLS & INGREDIENTS

Piping bags
Piping tips
Bain-marie
Offset spatulas
Palette knives
Stencils
Food coloring
Sprinkles
Luster dust

FUNDAMENTAL RECIPES: BUTTERCREAMS & BATTERS

*T*he buttercream is as important to a great cupcake as the batter, and it is much trickier to pull off. Buttercreams possess slightly different sweetness levels and fat ratios, one has to not only make them but account for their texture, mouthfeel, and pipe-ability (is that a word?) As I have a cake business, my Big Fish Buttercream was developed to complement my style of baking—it's easy to batch out and work with, and I can control the temperature and consistency of it more easily than I can when working with other popular buttercreams. It is my go-to, but everyone has their own preference—find yours among those provided here and master it, and then you can start catering to other people's preferences. A few things to keep in mind when preparing a buttercream: the temperature of your room is very important, and do not rush the process—take your time, and let the ingredients do the work.

You'll need around 5 cups (approximately 1,000 grams) of buttercream to frost two dozen cupcakes, so I have tailored these recipes to produce at least that amount. Once you are familiar with the required techniques, you can make smaller or larger batches. Anything smaller than a half batch often results in the sugars just sitting at the bottom of the bowl and the eggs struggling to meet desired volumes. And as nothing is worse than an overflowing mixer, I'd suggest that your biggest batch of buttercream be no more than 1.5 times larger.

Other buttercream fundamentals:

◇ Starting with fresh, high-quality butter and eggs and pure extracts or flavorings goes a long way toward producing the best buttercream.

◇ Make sure that your butter is at room temperature before creaming it, or before incorporating it into a meringue. If it is too cold, it will break down all that beautiful volume you've worked to achieve, and after it splits and comes back together, it will be denser than preferred.

◇ Once you've measured your ingredients, start mixing the buttercream immediately. You do not want to add heat without agitation, which will happen in recipes that include egg yolks, raw sugars, and salt. If this mixture sits, the temperature will quickly rise and cause coagulation. On top of that, the raw sugars will pull water from the egg yolks (egg yolks are about 50 percent water) and dry them up. This adds too much liquid to the mixture, meaning the ideal ratios are now off, and you will not be able to produce a proper buttercream that features the silky quality you're after.

◇ Freshly prepared buttercream is easiest to work with for intricate piping and coloring, so use it immediately, on cooled cupcakes, for the best results.

◇ If adding food coloring, use oil- or gel-based varieties to produce vibrant hues without thinning the buttercream.

◇ Store buttercream in an airtight container in the refrigerator if not using it immediately. After refrigerating, bring it back to room temperature and whip it again before using to restore its creamy consistency. When I'm whipping a refrigerated ice cream, I also run the flame of a kitchen torch against the bowl to warm the fat solids and help them re-emulsify.

◇ Pooling eggs is a great way to improve your efficiency. Separating eggs one at a time is tedious, and creates potential for eggshells to make their way into your baked goods, for yolks to break, and other issues. To avoid this, I carefully crack my eggs into a wide, shallow bowl and then carefully scoop the yolks out.

◇ Make sure your mixer attachments and bowl are clean and free of all oil and grease. Certain fats will keep the eggs from building volume and "climbing" the bowl as you'd like.

Big Fish Buttercream

YIELD: 5 CUPS / **ACTIVE TIME:** 30 MINUTES / **TOTAL TIME:** 30 MINUTES

Rich, creamy, ivory, not overly sweet at all, and easy to work with. This recipe was created on a whim and essentially shaped my cake business. Finally, I thought, a buttercream that isn't too temperamental, and one I can eat a healthy amount of! PSA: it is not "healthy" by any means.

Because of the large amount of butter in this buttercream, although it needs to be room temperature, it should not be too soft. In the summertime, pull the butter from the refrigerator the day you are making it, maybe just a few hours before using. In the winter, I often pull my butter 1 to 2 days ahead of time.

INGREDIENTS

1 (scant) cup (187 g) sugar

¼ cup (63 ml) water

3 (165 g) eggs

1 teaspoon (4 g) vanilla paste

1 teaspoon (6 g) kosher salt

3¼ cups (750 g) unsalted butter

Place the sugar and water in a small saucepan and cook the mixture over medium heat until it reaches 240°F. Place the eggs in the work bowl of a stand mixer fitted with the whisk attachment and whip them on high. With the mixer running on medium, add the hot syrup in a slow stream.

Add the vanilla and salt and whip the mixture on high until it has doubled in volume and is pale and fluffy. Set the mixer to medium-low and add the butter in pinches. When all of the butter has been added, whip the buttercream on high until the butter has completely emulsified.

The first five recipes for the buttercreams are ordered from the least sweet to the most. A good way to determine this measure when using other recipes is to look at the ratio of fats to sugars. The Big Fish Buttercream will be richer and less sweet, whereas the American Buttercream will very much lead with its sweetness.

Italian Meringue Buttercream

YIELD: 6¼ CUPS / **ACTIVE TIME:** 30 MINUTES / **TOTAL TIME:** 30 MINUTES

This is the most stable meringue there is, and this recipe will give you a sturdy, bright white base, silky mouthfeel, and less sweet flavor than other common buttercreams. This is my favorite buttercream to use if I'm working with a challenging color palette, or working in high humidity.

This is another buttercream that would benefit from a few minutes in the fridge or freezer before adding your butter. The meringue at this stage has generated so much volume, and even though the bowl may feel cool to the touch, the internal temperature of your meringue may be higher. It's much easier to be patient during these steps versus fixing a completely broken buttercream.

INGREDIENTS

2 (scant) cups (354 g) sugar

⅘ cup (176 ml) water

6 (207 g) large egg whites

1½ teaspoons (6 g) vanilla paste

Pinch of kosher salt

2¼ cups (531 g) unsalted butter, softened

Place the sugar and water in a small saucepan and cook the mixture over medium heat until it reaches 240°F. When the syrup is 220°F, place the egg whites in the work bowl of a stand mixer fitted with the whisk attachment and whip them on medium-high until a small bubble starts to form in them and you can no longer see raw egg whites on the bottom of the work bowl. The mixture will be a pale yellow with lots of bubbles. Turn the mixer to high and add the hot syrup in a slow stream. Whip until the mixture is completely cool and the meringue is bright white, 10 to 15 minutes.

Add the vanilla and salt and whip to incorporate. Set the mixer to medium-low and add the butter in pinches. When all of the butter has been added, whip the buttercream on high until the butter has completely emulsified.

French Meringue Buttercream

YIELD: 5¼ CUPS / **ACTIVE TIME:** 30 MINUTES / **TOTAL TIME:** 30 MINUTES

This is soooo yummy. But I love fat, and in truth, this buttercream is way too rich for most of my clients, so I do not make it often. But for personal use, this is my second choice after the Big Fish Buttercream. It is heavy but smooth and pairs well with more decadent cake flavors. I've found that it's better in cooler seasons and does not do well in warmer weather. It is also the darkest buttercream, so if you are looking for pale colors, I advise you to use the Italian Meringue Buttercream or Swiss Meringue Buttercream (see page 29 or 31).

This recipe is way less forgiving if the sugar is not cooked properly, since the high percentage of fats creates potential for coagulation if the sugar gets overcooked, and there will be less opportunity to create air bubbles if the sugar is undercooked. You also may find that this recipe takes a little longer to emulsify, so popping it in the refrigerator for 5 to 10 minutes if the butter looks to be too greasy or seems to be melting is a good idea. After that brief chill, put it right back on the mixer.

INGREDIENTS

1½ cups (300 g) sugar

3 (165 g) eggs

6 (100 g) egg yolks

2 teaspoons (8 g) vanilla paste

Pinch of kosher salt

2 cups (454 g) unsalted butter, softened

Place the sugar in a small saucepan and cook it over medium heat until it reaches 240°F. Place the eggs and egg yolks in the work bowl of a stand mixer fitted with the whisk attachment and whip them on high until they are pale and fluffy, about 5 minutes. With the mixer running on medium-low, add the hot sugar in a slow stream.

Add the vanilla and salt and whip the mixture on medium-low. Add the butter in pinches. When all of the butter has been added, whip the buttercream on medium-high until the butter has completely emulsified, about 7 minutes.

Swiss Meringue Buttercream

YIELD: 6¼ CUPS / **ACTIVE TIME:** 30 MINUTES / **TOTAL TIME:** 30 MINUTES

This is an industry favorite. Its bright white is perfect for weddings, it's a bit on the sweeter side, takes on colors really well, and pipes beautifully. That said, I do not use it too often because I make huge batches of buttercream at a time and this buttercream has a few tricky steps and requires more equipment, keeping me from moving as fast as I need to. But when I'm making a cupcake set for a kid's birthday, I usually start here, as it is very easy to flavor and has a nice, silky mouthfeel that kids love.

If the buttercream seems too soft after adding the butter, place the bowl in the refrigerator for a few minutes. This will help cool down those solids so that when you return the buttercream to the mixer the volume will increase. Whip for another minute or so, until there are no lumps and the buttercream is smooth and pipable.

INGREDIENTS

7½ (287 g) egg whites

2½ cups (500 g) sugar

2½ teaspoons (10 g) vanilla paste

Pinch of kosher salt

1⅘ cups (437 g) unsalted butter, softened

Fill a medium saucepan halfway with water and bring to a simmer. Place the egg whites, sugar, and vanilla in the work bowl of a stand mixer, place it over the simmering water, making sure the bottom of the bowl is not touching the water, and whisk continually until the mixture is 160°F. Place the bowl on the stand mixer, fit it with the whisk attachment, and whip on high speed until the mixture holds stiff peaks and has cooled completely, 10 to 15 minutes.

Fit the mixer with the paddle attachment, add the salt, and beat on low to incorporate. Add the butter in pinches, raise the speed to medium, and beat, gradually raising the speed to high as the buttercream starts to emulsify. When the buttercream is light, white, and very fluffy, it is ready.

American Buttercream

YIELD: 5½ CUPS / **ACTIVE TIME:** 20 MINUTES / **TOTAL TIME:** 20 MINUTES

In true Gabby fashion, I took a traditional American Buttercream recipe and adapted it over time to have ... you guessed it ... twice the amount of butter it actually needs. This makes the buttercream feel silky and whipped and gives it a bright white hue. This is the perfect base to start learning how to mix in colors and practice your piping skills.

INGREDIENTS

2½ cups (560 g) unsalted butter, softened

4 cups (498 g) confectioners' sugar, sifted

½ teaspoon (2 g) vanilla paste

Pinch of kosher salt

4¾ teaspoons (20 ml) heavy cream

Place the butter and confectioners' sugar in the work bowl of a stand mixer fitted with the paddle attachment and beat on medium-high until the mixture is pale and fluffy, about 8 minutes.

Reduce the speed to medium, add the vanilla paste, salt, and heavy cream, and beat until the buttercream is bright white and fluffy, about 5 minutes.

Vegan Buttercream

YIELD: 5 CUPS / **ACTIVE TIME:** 20 MINUTES / **TOTAL TIME:** 20 MINUTES

Vegan baking is a whole other ballgame. It is no easy task, challenging to adapt and manipulate, and personally not my strong suit. But I do have clients who ask for it, so this is my base buttercream for those occasions. I do have limitations when it comes to specialty decorating because this base buttercream just does not act the same way as others do. I'm also limited in terms of adding flavors because the frosting is incredibly fragile. I have to work fast when piping it, as the vegan butter, which is essentially just oil, quickly melts from the heat of my hands. However, if you need to supply a bit of plant-based indulgence, I think this buttercream is as close as you're going to get to the real deal. I highly encourage you to practice with this one a lot before sharing your efforts with others.

I prefer to use whipped vegan butter, as I feel it already has a good amount of air in it and thus is easier to emulsify.

INGREDIENTS

2 cups (474 g) whipped vegan butter

6½ cups (780 g) confectioners' sugar, sifted

2 teaspoons (8 g) vanilla paste

¼ teaspoon (1.5 g) kosher salt

1 tablespoon (15 ml) oat milk

Place the butter and confectioners' sugar in the work bowl of a stand mixer fitted with the paddle attachment and beat on medium-high until the mixture is light and fluffy, 4 to 6 minutes.

Reduce the speed to medium, add the vanilla paste, salt, and oat milk, and beat until the buttercream is just combined.

Vanilla Cupcake Batter

YIELD: 36 CUPCAKES / **ACTIVE TIME:** 25 MINUTES / TOTAL TIME: 50 MINUTES

This is my go-to recipe for cupcakes, as it's a great base to add flavors to. This recipe in particular is great for wedding cupcakes, and is easy to batch out on a larger scale, since it is sturdy, moist, has a tight crumb structure, and a good shelf life.

INGREDIENTS

6 (330 g) eggs

2⅔ cups (538 g) sugar

2 tablespoons (26 g) vanilla paste

4⅓ cups (600 g) cake flour

3¼ teaspoons (15 g) baking powder

Pinch of kosher salt

2⅔ cups (625 ml) heavy cream

In the work bowl of a stand mixer fitted with the whisk attachment, whip the eggs, sugar, and vanilla on high until the mixture has doubled in volume, 5 to 7 minutes.

Place the flour, baking powder, and salt in a mixing bowl and whisk to combine. Sift the mixture through a fine-mesh tamis onto a piece of parchment paper. Fold the parchment paper lengthwise and alternate between adding small increments of the dry mixture and heavy cream to the work bowl, folding to incorporate each addition and scraping down the work bowl as needed.

While there are many cupcake batters in the following pages, these recipes serve as the bases for the majority of the cupcakes I make at Big Fish.

White Cupcake Batter

YIELD: 36 CUPCAKES / ACTIVE TIME: 25 MINUTES / TOTAL TIME: 50 MINUTES

This batter is a client favorite as it is bright white inside, light, and fluffy. Think angel food, but with a bit more muscle. When building wedding cakes I can't have anything unstable, so I offer this recipe for clients wanting that softer cake texture, and have found that it's especially great for summertime weddings. For a cupcake, this batter does tend to pull off the liners a bit, so pinning down the proper oven temperature and baking times for your oven are ideal here. I also like to let this batter rest in the liners for 5 to 10 minutes before baking.

INGREDIENTS

1 cup (230 g) unsalted butter, softened

1¾ cups (370 g) sugar

Pinch of kosher salt

2¾ cups (384 g) cake flour

2 teaspoons (10 g) baking powder

2 tablespoons (26 g) vanilla paste

1 cup (244 ml) whole milk

2 tablespoons (28 g) sour cream

3 (113 g) egg whites

In the work bowl of a stand mixer fitted with the paddle attachment, cream the butter, three-quarters of the sugar, and the salt on high until the mixture is light and fluffy, about 5 minutes.

Place the flour and baking powder in a bowl and whisk to combine. Sift the mixture through a fine-mesh tamis onto a piece of parchment paper. Fold the parchment paper lengthwise and alternate adding small increments of the dry mixture and vanilla, milk, and sour cream to the work bowl, folding to incorporate each addition and scraping down the work bowl as needed. Transfer the batter to a separate large mixing bowl, cover it with a kitchen towel, and wash the work bowl of the stand mixer.

Fit the stand mixer with the whisk attachment and whip the egg whites on medium, slowly adding the remaining sugar, until the mixture is bright, glossy, and has increased in volume considerably. Gently fold the whipped egg whites into the batter until fully incorporated.

Butter Cupcake Batter

YIELD: 24 CUPCAKES / **ACTIVE TIME:** 25 MINUTES / **TOTAL TIME:** 50 MINUTES

One for all of the yellow cake fans out there. The color is due to the ramped-up fat content, but it is also a touch sweeter than the other vanilla-centered batters because of the brown sugar. The canola oil here makes this recipe moist and bouncy. This is also a very versatile recipe, which I use a lot in the cooler months because I find it warming.

INGREDIENTS

5¾ tablespoons (82.5 g) unsalted butter, softened

⅓ cup (75 g) Crisco

1⅔ cups (318.5 g) sugar

¼ cup (56 g) brown sugar

4 (220 g) eggs

⅓ cup (75 ml) canola oil

2⅓ cups (315 g) cake flour

1⅔ teaspoons (7.5 g) baking powder

½ cup (135 ml) whole milk

In the work bowl of a stand mixer fitted with the paddle attachment, cream the butter, Crisco, sugar, and brown sugar on high until the mixture is pale and fluffy, about 5 minutes.

Add the eggs one at a time and beat to incorporate. With the mixer running on medium, add the canola oil in a slow stream and beat to incorporate.

Scrape down the work bowl. Place the flour and baking powder in a separate mixing bowl and whisk to combine. Sift the mixture through a fine-mesh tamis onto a piece of parchment paper. Fold the parchment paper lengthwise. Add one-third of the dry mixture to the work bowl, beat to incorporate, add half of the milk, and beat to incorporate. Repeat with another third of the dry mixture and the remaining milk. Add the remaining dry mixture and beat until the batter just comes together. Scrape down the work bowl as needed while adding the dry mixture and milk.

Vegan & Gluten-Free Cupcake Batter

YIELD: 24 CUPCAKES / **ACTIVE TIME:** 25 MINUTES / **TOTAL TIME:** 50 MINUTES

Make sure you check out my advice on preparing gluten-free baked goods in the Essential Techniques & Tools chapter.

INGREDIENTS

16.2 oz. (460 ml) oat milk

4.9 oz. (140 ml) canola oil

1¾ oz. (50 g) vanilla paste

⅓ oz. (12 ml) fresh lemon juice

12.7 oz. (360 g) all-purpose flour

11.3 oz. (320 g) sugar

3½ oz. (100 g) brown sugar

⅓ oz. (10 g) kosher salt

1 teaspoon (4 g) baking powder

Place the oat milk, canola oil, vanilla paste, and lemon juice in a mixing bowl and whisk to combine.

Place the flour, sugar, brown sugar, salt, and baking powder in a mixing bowl and whisk to combine. Make a well in the center of the dry mixture, pour the wet mixture into the well, and whisk until the resulting mixture just comes together as a batter.

Chocolate Cupcake Batter

YIELD: 30 CUPCAKES / **ACTIVE TIME:** 25 MINUTES / **TOTAL TIME:** 50 MINUTES

If you, or someone close to you, is a choco-holic, this recipe will seem descended from on high.

INGREDIENTS

3 (156 g) eggs

2¼ cups (450 g) sugar

¾ cup (175 ml) canola oil

1¼ cups (107 g) cocoa powder

1¾ cups (250 g) cake flour

2 teaspoons (8.5 g) baking powder

⅔ cup (157 ml) heavy cream

1¼ cups (300 ml) whole milk

In the work bowl of a stand mixer fitted with the whisk attachment, whip the eggs, sugar, and canola oil on high until the mixture is pale and fluffy, about 5 minutes.

Scrape down the work bowl. Place the cocoa powder, flour, and baking powder in a separate mixing bowl and whisk to combine. Place the cream and milk in a separate mixing bowl and stir to combine. Sift the mixture through a fine-mesh tamis onto a piece of parchment paper. Fold the parchment paper lengthwise. Add one-third of the dry mixture to the work bowl, whip to incorporate, add half of the milk mixture, and whip to incorporate. Repeat with another third of the dry mixture and the remaining milk mixture. Add the remaining dry mixture and beat until the batter just comes together. Scrape down the work bowl as needed while adding the mixtures.

WEDDINGS & OTHER SPECIAL OCCASIONS

*I*n my business, weddings are the primary mover, the events that produce many of the long days, creativity that captures something unique about the customers, and, blessedly, revenue. And while these cupcake recipes can work at any time, you can trust that they will provide the magic you're looking for when everything has to be extraordinary.

While weddings are wonderful, they are not the only special occasion worthy of celebrating with a special, bespoke confection. This chapter also has recipes and ideas for those instances, helping you guarantee that those magical moments become lasting memories.

White Chocolate & Raspberry Cupcakes

YIELD: 36 CUPCAKES / **ACTIVE TIME:** 20 MINUTES / **TOTAL TIME:** 50 MINUTES

Cheers to one of the most celebrated flavor combinations in the world of weddings today. These cupcakes are feminine, dainty, capable of versatile decoration, work in any season, have a clean and elegant beauty, and balanced flavor. For the modern couple that respects traditions, these cupcakes have the ideal character, one that will be cherished and remembered by all your guests.

INGREDIENTS

White Cupcake Batter
(see page 35)

FOR THE FILLING

¾ cup (174 g) The Perfect Puree Raspberry Puree

1 teaspoon (5 ml) fresh lemon juice

⅙ cup (33 g) sugar

2 tablespoons (16 g) cornstarch

FOR THE BUTTERCREAM

Big Fish Buttercream
(see page 28)

¾ cup (105 g) melted white chocolate (28 percent white chocolate), cooled to 90°F

Preheat the oven to 325°F on convection mode or 350°F for a conventional oven. Line three cupcake pans with paper liners.

Prepare the batter, transfer it to a piping bag, and pipe it into the paper liners. Place the cupcakes in the oven and bake until their internal temperature is 200°F, 20 to 25 minutes, rotating the pans halfway through.

To prepare the filling, place the raspberry puree and lemon juice in a small saucepan and warm the mixture over medium heat. In a small bowl, whisk the sugar and cornstarch together, add the mixture to the pan, and whisk continually until the coulis has thickened, about 2 minutes. Transfer the coulis to a bowl and place plastic wrap directly on the surface to prevent a skin from forming. Let the coulis cool to room temperature.

Remove the cupcakes from the oven and let them rest in the pans for 5 minutes. Using an offset spatula, remove the cupcakes from the pans and transfer them to a cupcake holder. Cover them tightly and let them cool completely.

When the cupcakes have cooled completely and are ready to be frosted, prepare the Big Fish Buttercream. With the mixer running, add the white chocolate and beat until it has emulsified. Set the buttercream aside.

Working from the tops of the cupcakes, remove their centers and fill them with the coulis. Frost the cupcakes with the white chocolate buttercream and serve.

Vanilla Bean Cupcakes

YIELD: 36 CUPCAKES / **ACTIVE TIME:** 20 MINUTES / **TOTAL TIME:** 50 MINUTES

I have used many forms of vanilla in my baking career, and have finally settled on Tahitian vanilla paste. It is more aromatic than other varieties, but I find it's still rich enough to complement the amount of fat I tend to use in my baking. It's sweet, it's smooth, and the paste I use does not have added alcohol, so you can use as much as you want without worrying about the bitter aftertaste. A true game changer that's well worth seeking out.

INGREDIENTS

Vanilla Cupcake Batter
(see page 34)

Italian Meringue
Buttercream (see page 29)

Preheat the oven to 325°F on convection mode or 350°F for a conventional oven. Line three cupcake pans with paper liners.

Prepare the batter, transfer it to a piping bag, and pipe it into the paper liners. Place the cupcakes in the oven and bake until their internal temperature is 200°F, 20 to 25 minutes, rotating the pans halfway through.

Remove the cupcakes from the oven and let them rest in the pans for 5 minutes. Using an offset spatula, remove the cupcakes from the pans and transfer them to a cupcake holder. Cover them tightly and let them cool completely.

When the cupcakes have cooled completely and are ready to be frosted, prepare the buttercream.

Frost the cupcakes with the buttercream and serve.

Champagne Cupcakes

YIELD: 24 CUPCAKES / **ACTIVE TIME:** 20 MINUTES / **TOTAL TIME:** 50 MINUTES

In times of celebration, people turn to Champagne, which they say has positive effects on a woman's beauty, and a man's wit. Apropos for the modern wedding, if you ask me.

Preheat the oven to 325°F on convection mode or 350°F for a conventional oven. Line two cupcake pans with paper liners.

To begin preparations for the cupcakes, place the flour, sugar, baking powder, baking soda, and salt in a mixing bowl and whisk to combine. Sift the mixture through a fine-mesh tamis into the work bowl of a stand mixer fitted with the paddle attachment, add the butter, and beat until the mixture is sandy, about 1 minute.

Add the buttermilk and canola oil and beat on medium for about 5 minutes.

Scrape down the work bowl, add the egg whites, Champagne, vanilla, and food coloring, and beat until the mixture comes together as a smooth batter, about 2 minutes.

Transfer the batter to a piping bag and pipe it into the paper liners. Place the cupcakes in the oven and bake until their internal temperature is 200°F, 20 to 25 minutes, rotating the pans halfway through.

Remove the cupcakes from the oven and let them rest in the pans for 5 minutes. Using an offset spatula, remove the cupcakes from the pans and transfer them to a cupcake holder. Cover them tightly and let them cool completely.

While the cupcakes are cooling, prepare the buttercream. Place the Champagne in a small saucepan and bring it to a boil over medium heat. Cook until it has reduced to ½ cup. Remove the pan from heat and let the Champagne cool to room temperature. Place the butter in the work bowl of a stand mixer fitted with the paddle attachment and beat until it is pale and fluffy, about 5 minutes. With the mixer running on low speed, add the confectioners' sugar in small increments and beat to incorporate, scraping down the work bowl as needed. Add the reduced Champagne, vanilla, and salt and beat on high until the buttercream is emulsified, about 3 minutes.

Frost the cupcakes with the Champagne buttercream and serve.

INGREDIENTS

FOR THE CUPCAKES

2⅔ cups (368 g) cake flour

1⅓ cups (283 g) sugar

1 tablespoon (13 g) baking powder

½ teaspoon (2 g) baking soda

½ teaspoon (3 g) kosher salt

¾ cup (170 g) unsalted butter, softened

½ cup (113 ml) buttermilk

¼ cup (56 ml) canola oil

3 (113 g) egg whites

¾ cup (170 ml) Champagne

1 teaspoon (4 g) vanilla paste

Drop of pink food coloring

FOR THE BUTTERCREAM

1½ cups (340 ml) Champagne

2¼ cups (510 g) unsalted butter, softened

7½ cups (900 g) confectioners' sugar, sifted

1 tablespoon (12 g) vanilla paste

Pinch of kosher salt

INGREDIENTS

FOR THE CUPCAKES

Vanilla Cupcake Batter
(see page 34)

Zest of 2 oranges

1½ teaspoons (7.5 ml)
orange blossom extract

FOR THE FILLING

¾ sheet (1.9 g) of silver
gelatin

½ cup (108 ml) orange juice

2 (108 g) eggs

½ cup (108 g) sugar

9¾ tablespoons (140 g)
unsalted butter

FOR THE BUTTERCREAM

1 (scant) cup (187 g) honey

3 (165 g) eggs

1¾ teaspoons (8 g) vanilla
paste

Pinch of kosher salt

3¼ cups (750 g) unsalted
butter, softened

Orange Blossom Cupcakes

YIELD: 36 CUPCAKES / **ACTIVE TIME:** 20 MINUTES / **TOTAL TIME:** 50 MINUTES

These cupcakes combine the delicate flavor of orange blossom and the floral sweetness of a honey-spiked buttercream.

Preheat the oven to 325°F on convection mode or 350°F for a conventional oven. Line three cupcake pans with paper liners.

To begin preparations for the cupcakes, prepare the batter, adding the orange zest and orange blossom extract toward the end of the mixing process. Transfer the batter to a piping bag and pipe the batter into the paper liners. Place the cupcakes in the oven and bake until their internal temperature is 200°F, 20 to 25 minutes, rotating the pans halfway through.

To prepare the filling, place the gelatin in a bowl of water and let it bloom. Place the orange juice, eggs, and sugar in a small saucepan and warm the mixture over medium heat, whisking continually, until it reaches 170°F and starts to thicken. Strain the mixture into a blender, add the bloomed gelatin and butter, and puree until smooth. Transfer the curd to a small bowl and place plastic wrap directly on the surface to prevent a skin from forming. Let the curd cool completely.

Remove the cupcakes from the oven and let them rest in the pans for 5 minutes. Using an offset spatula, remove the cupcakes from the pans and transfer them to a cupcake holder. Cover them tightly and let them cool completely.

To prepare the buttercream, place the honey in a small saucepan and cook it over medium heat until it reaches 240°F. Place the eggs in the work bowl of a stand mixer fitted with the whisk attachment and whip them on high. With the mixer running at medium, add the hot honey in a slow stream. Add the vanilla and salt and whip the mixture on high until it has doubled in volume and is pale and fluffy. Set the mixer to medium-low and add the butter in pinches. When all of the butter has been added, whip the buttercream on high until the butter has completely emulsified.

Working from the tops of the cupcakes, remove their centers and fill them with the curd. Frost the cupcakes with the honey buttercream and serve.

Graduation Day Cupcakes

YIELD: 36 CUPCAKES / **ACTIVE TIME:** 20 MINUTES / **TOTAL TIME:** 50 MINUTES

When deciding how to decorate these cupcakes, focus on the school's colors first, then try to articulate elements of the specific field of study.

INGREDIENTS

White Cupcake Batter
(see page 35)

White chocolate
buttercream (see page 42)

Drops of preferred food
coloring

Preheat the oven to 325°F on convection mode or 350°F for a conventional oven. Line three cupcake pans with paper liners.

Prepare the batter, transfer it to a piping bag, and pipe it into the paper liners. Place the cupcakes in the oven and bake until their internal temperature is 200°F, 20 to 25 minutes, rotating the pans halfway through.

Remove the cupcakes from the oven and let them rest in the pans for 5 minutes. Using an offset spatula, remove the cupcakes from the pans and transfer them to a cupcake holder. Cover them tightly and let them cool completely.

Prepare the buttercream and divide it between two bowls. Add one of your chosen food colorings to each of the bowls and beat to incorporate them.

Frost the cupcakes with the white chocolate buttercream and serve.

Almond Cupcakes

YIELD: 18 CUPCAKES / **ACTIVE TIME:** 20 MINUTES / **TOTAL TIME:** 50 MINUTES

Symbolizing good luck, fertility, and new beginnings, almond cake has remained one of the top wedding flavors for generations, and I don't see it going anywhere anytime soon.

INGREDIENTS

FOR THE CUPCAKES

1⅓ cups (265 g) sugar

¾ cup (225 g) almond paste

1⅛ cups (140 g) all-purpose flour

1½ teaspoons (7 g) baking powder

¾ teaspoon (4 g) kosher salt

1 cup (225 g) unsalted butter, softened

1 teaspoon (4 g) vanilla paste

1 teaspoon (5 ml) almond extract

6 (330 g) eggs

FOR THE BUTTERCREAM

American Buttercream (see page 32)

1 tablespoon (15 ml) almond extract

Preheat the oven to 325°F on convection mode or 350°F in a conventional oven. Line two cupcake pans with paper liners.

To begin preparations for the cupcakes, place the sugar and almond paste in a food processor and blitz until the mixture is smooth, about 1 minute. Place the flour, baking powder, and salt in a bowl and whisk to combine. Sift the mixture through a fine-mesh tamis onto a piece of parchment paper. Fold the parchment paper lengthwise, add the mixture to the food processor in three increments, and pulse to incorporate, about 30 seconds for each increment.

Add the butter, vanilla paste, and almond extract and pulse until the mixture is smooth, 2 to 3 minutes. Add the eggs one at a time and pulse until the batter is smooth and homogenous after each addition.

Transfer the batter to a piping bag and pipe the batter into the paper liners. Place the cupcakes in the oven and bake until their internal temperature is 200°F, 20 to 25 minutes, rotating the pans halfway through.

Remove the cupcakes from the oven and let them rest in the pans for 5 minutes. Using an offset spatula, remove the cupcakes from the pans and transfer them to a cupcake holder. Cover them tightly and let them cool completely.

When the cupcakes have cooled completely and are ready to be frosted, prepare the American Buttercream. With the mixer running, add the almond extract to the buttercream and beat until it has been incorporated.

Frost the cupcakes with the almond buttercream and serve.

Birthday Cupcakes

YIELD: 36 CUPCAKES / **ACTIVE TIME:** 20 MINUTES / **TOTAL TIME:** 50 MINUTES

It's the best day of the year to enjoy a cupcake—bonus if you got someone else to bake these Funfetti-style cupcakes for you!

INGREDIENTS

White Cupcake Batter
(see page 35)

1 cup rainbow sprinkles

American Buttercream
(see page 32)

Preheat the oven to 325°F on convection mode or 350°F in a conventional oven. Line three cupcake pans with paper liners.

Prepare the batter, adding the sprinkles toward the end of the mixing process. Transfer the batter to a piping bag and pipe it into the paper liners. Place the cupcakes in the oven and bake until their internal temperature is 200°F, 20 to 25 minutes, rotating the pans halfway through.

Remove the cupcakes from the oven and let them rest in the pans for 5 minutes. Using an offset spatula, remove the cupcakes from the pans and transfer them to a cupcake holder. Cover them tightly and let them cool completely.

When the cupcakes have cooled completely and are ready to be frosted, prepare the buttercream.

Frost the cupcakes with the buttercream and serve.

INGREDIENTS

FOR THE CUPCAKES

1½ cups (300 g) sugar

1½ cups (327 ml) canola oil

2 (110 g) eggs

2½ cups (342 g) cake flour

2 tablespoons (11 g) cocoa powder

1 teaspoon (6 g) kosher salt

1½ teaspoons (7 g) baking soda

2 teaspoons (10 g) distilled vinegar

1 cup (238 ml) buttermilk

½ teaspoon (2 g) red food coloring

1 teaspoon (4 g) vanilla paste

FOR THE BUTTERCREAM

1 cup (227 g) unsalted butter, softened

1½ cups (340 g) cream cheese, softened

4 cups (454 g) confectioners' sugar

¾ teaspoon (3 g) vanilla paste

Pinch of citric acid

Anniversary Cupcakes

YIELD: 36 CUPCAKES / **ACTIVE TIME:** 20 MINUTES / **TOTAL TIME:** 50 MINUTES

Even if you forget, you probably have everything you need already and can whip these up quickly. Thoughtfulness on the fly.

Preheat the oven to 325°F on convection mode or 350°F in a conventional oven. Line three cupcake pans with paper liners.

To begin preparations for the cupcakes, place the sugar and canola oil in the work bowl of a stand mixer fitted with the whisk attachment and whip on high until the mixture is fluffy, 3 to 5 minutes. Add the eggs one at a time and whip to incorporate.

Place the flour, cocoa powder, and salt in a mixing bowl and whisk to combine. Sift the mixture through a fine-mesh tamis onto a piece of parchment paper and set it aside. Place the baking soda and vinegar in a mixing bowl and whisk to combine. The mixture will foam a little bit. Set it aside.

Fold the parchment paper in half lengthwise. With the mixer running, alternate between adding small increments of the dry mixture and buttermilk to the work bowl, scraping down the work bowl as needed. Add the food coloring, vanilla, and baking soda mixture and whip until the resulting mixture just comes together as a smooth batter. Transfer the red velvet cupcake batter to a piping bag and pipe it into the paper liners.

Place the cupcakes in the oven and bake until their internal temperature is 200°F, 20 to 25 minutes, rotating the pans halfway through.

Remove the cupcakes from the oven and let them rest in the pans for 5 minutes. Using an offset spatula, remove the cupcakes from the pans and transfer them to a cupcake holder. Cover them tightly and let them cool completely.

When the cupcakes have cooled completely and are ready to be frosted, prepare the buttercream. Place the butter and cream cheese in the work bowl of a stand mixer fitted with the paddle attachment and beat until the mixture is fluffy and clump-free, 5 to 7 minutes. Scrape down the work bowl, add the confectioners' sugar ½ cup at a time, and beat on medium to incorporate. When all of the sugar has been added, set the mixer to high, add the vanilla and citric acid, and beat until the buttercream is smooth.

Frost the cupcakes with the cream cheese buttercream and serve.

Carrot Cupcakes

YIELD: 24 CUPCAKES / **ACTIVE TIME:** 20 MINUTES / **TOTAL TIME:** 50 MINUTES

The first published recipe for carrot cake likely came in a 1929 cookbook, *The 20th-Century Bride's Cookbook*. The recipe wasn't a hit initially, but has now become a classic in American wedding culture.

INGREDIENTS

2 cups (398 g) sugar

1 cup (205 ml) canola oil

4 (220 g) eggs

2½ cups (309 g) all-purpose flour

¾ teaspoon (4 g) baking powder

1½ teaspoons (9 g) baking soda

Pinch of kosher salt

1½ tablespoons (11 g) Spice Girl Mix (see page 254)

1 cup (117 g) chopped walnuts

1 cup (165 g) minced pineapple

2 cups (232 g) shredded carrots

Cream cheese buttercream (see page 57)

Preheat the oven to 325°F on convection mode or 350°F in a conventional oven. Line two cupcake pans with paper liners.

Place the sugar, canola oil, and eggs in the work bowl of a stand mixer fitted with the whisk attachment and whip on high until the mixture has doubled in volume, 3 to 5 minutes.

Place the flour, baking powder, baking soda, salt, and Spice Girl Mix in a mixing bowl and whisk to combine. Sift the mixture through a fine-mesh tamis onto a piece of parchment paper. Fold the parchment paper lengthwise.

With the mixer running, add small increments of the dry mixture into the work bowl, scraping down the work bowl as needed. Add the walnuts, pineapple, and carrots and fold to incorporate. Transfer the batter to a piping bag and pipe it into the paper liners.

Place the cupcakes in the oven and bake until their internal temperature is 200°F, 20 to 25 minutes, rotating the pans halfway through.

Remove the cupcakes from the oven and let them rest in the pans for 5 minutes. Using an offset spatula, remove the cupcakes from the pans and transfer them to a cupcake holder. Cover them tightly and let them cool completely.

When the cupcakes have cooled completely and are ready to be frosted, prepare the buttercream.

Frost the cupcakes with the cream cheese buttercream and serve.

Rose Cupcakes

YIELD: 36 CUPCAKES / **ACTIVE TIME:** 20 MINUTES / **TOTAL TIME:** 50 MINUTES

There is something classic, romantic, and bold about the combination of rose water and pistachio, a happy union that makes these cupcakes perfect for a garden wedding.

INGREDIENTS

FOR THE CUPCAKES

White Cupcake Batter
(see page 35)

2 tablespoons (30 ml)
rose water

1 tablespoon rose petals

FOR THE BUTTERCREAM

American Buttercream
(see page 32)

2 teaspoons (10 ml)
rose water

Preheat the oven to 325°F on convection mode or 350°F for a conventional oven. Line three cupcake pans with paper liners.

To begin preparations for the cupcakes, prepare the batter, adding the rose water and rose petals toward the end of the mixing process. Transfer it to a piping bag and pipe the batter into the paper liners.

Place the cupcakes in the oven and bake until their internal temperature is 200°F, 20 to 25 minutes, rotating the pans halfway through.

Remove the cupcakes from the oven and let them rest in the pans for 5 minutes. Using an offset spatula, remove the cupcakes from the pans and transfer them to a cupcake holder. Cover them tightly and let them cool completely.

When the cupcakes have cooled completely and are ready to be frosted, prepare the American Buttercream. With the mixer running, add the rose water to the buttercream and beat until it has been incorporated.

Frost the cupcakes with the rose buttercream and serve.

Coconut Cupcakes

YIELD: 36 CUPCAKES / **ACTIVE TIME:** 20 MINUTES / **TOTAL TIME:** 50 MINUTES

Here's a year-round favorite that is great for crowds, and such a brilliant white that it goes beautifully with the bride's dress.

INGREDIENTS

White Cupcake Batter
(see page 35)

2 cups (186 g) sweetened
coconut flakes

Big Fish Buttercream
(see page 28)

Unsweetened coconut
flakes, toasted, for topping

Preheat the oven to 325°F on convection mode or 350°F in a conventional oven. Line three cupcake pans with paper liners.

Prepare the batter, adding the sweetened coconut flakes toward the end of the mixing process. Transfer the batter to a piping bag and pipe it into the paper liners. Place the cupcakes in the oven and bake until their internal temperature is 200°F, 20 to 25 minutes, rotating the pans halfway through.

Remove the cupcakes from the oven and let them rest in the pans for 5 minutes. Using an offset spatula, remove the cupcakes from the pans and transfer them to a cupcake holder. Cover them tightly and let them cool completely.

When the cupcakes have cooled completely and are ready to be frosted, prepare the buttercream.

Frost the cupcakes with the buttercream, top them with some toasted coconut, and serve.

COCONUT CUPCAKES, SEE PAGE 61

Marble Cupcakes

YIELD: 36 CUPCAKES / **ACTIVE TIME:** 20 MINUTES / **TOTAL TIME:** 50 MINUTES

Cupcakes that supply the best of both worlds, and provide mesmerizing swirls of chocolate and vanilla. These cupcakes are perfect for a group of picky people, as they are assured to have something they like.

INGREDIENTS

Vanilla Cupcake Batter
(see page 34)

⅓ cup (28 g) cocoa powder

¼ cup (59 ml) boiling water

Big Fish Buttercream
(see page 28)

½ lb. (227 g) milk chocolate, melted and cooled to 90°F

Preheat the oven to 325°F on convection mode or 350°F in a conventional oven. Line three cupcake pans with paper liners.

Prepare the batter and reserve 1 cup. Place the reserved batter, cocoa powder, and boiling water in a mixing bowl and whisk to combine. Transfer each batter to its own piping bag and pipe the batters into the paper liners, swirling them.

Place the cupcakes in the oven and bake until their internal temperature is 200°F, 20 to 25 minutes, rotating the pans halfway through.

Remove the cupcakes from the oven and let them rest in the pans for 5 minutes. Using an offset spatula, remove the cupcakes from the pans and transfer them to a cupcake holder. Cover them tightly and let them cool completely.

When the cupcakes have cooled completely and are ready to be frosted, prepare the buttercream and place half of it in a separate bowl. Add the melted chocolate to one portion of the buttercream and beat until it is incorporated.

Frost the cupcakes with the chocolate buttercream and Big Fish Buttercream and serve.

Bridal Shower Cupcakes

YIELD: 30 CUPCAKES / **ACTIVE TIME:** 30 MINUTES / **TOTAL TIME:** 24 HOURS

When decorating cupcakes for any pre-bridal event I love looking at the wedding details. Playing with the couple's color scheme or a party theme is a fun way to extend the festivities and tie everything together. These were for a real client, who held her shower in a garden.

The day before you are going to prepare the cupcakes, place the poppy seeds and milk in a bowl and let the poppy seeds soak in the refrigerator overnight.

Preheat the oven to 325°F on convection mode or 350°F in a conventional oven. Line three cupcake pans with paper liners.

Place the lemon juice and zest in a small saucepan and bring to a simmer over medium heat. Cook until the mixture has reduced and becomes syrupy, about 10 minutes. Remove the pan from heat and let the syrup cool.

Place the eggs and sugar in the work bowl of a stand mixer fitted with the whisk attachment and whip on high until the mixture is light and fluffy, about 6 minutes. With the mixer running, add the canola oil in a slow stream. Add the vanilla and lemon syrup and whip to incorporate.

Place the flour and baking powder in a bowl and whisk to combine. Sift the mixture through a fine-mesh tamis onto a piece of parchment paper. Fold the parchment paper lengthwise. Alternate between adding small increments of the dry mixture and poppy seed mixture to the work bowl, folding to incorporate each addition and scraping down the work bowl as needed.

Transfer the batter to a piping bag, pipe it into the paper liners, and place the cupcakes in the oven. Bake until their internal temperature is 200°F, 20 to 25 minutes, rotating the pans halfway through.

Remove the cupcakes from the oven and let them rest in the pans for 5 minutes. Using an offset spatula, remove the cupcakes from the pans and transfer them to a cupcake holder. Cover them tightly and let them cool completely.

When the cupcakes have cooled completely and are ready to be frosted, prepare the buttercream.

Frost the cupcakes with the buttercream and serve.

INGREDIENTS

⅓ cup (53 g) poppy seeds

1¼ cups (300 ml) milk

⅔ cup (150 ml) fresh lemon juice

Zest of 3 to 4 large lemons

2½ (137 g) eggs

2⅛ cups (425 g) sugar

1 cup (218 ml) canola oil

2 teaspoons (9 g) vanilla paste

3½ cups (445 g) all-purpose flour

1 tablespoon (15 g) baking powder

Big Fish Buttercream (see page 28)

Congrats on Adulting Cupcakes

YIELD: 30 CUPCAKES / **ACTIVE TIME:** 25 MINUTES / **TOTAL TIME:** 50 MINUTES

Finally nailed down your morning routine, opened a Roth IRA, have a reliable car—that's adulting! And it should be celebrated, as should any instance when you level up. When I was fresh out of college and starting out in professional kitchens, I moved back in with my parents. When I finally moved out my brother-in-law bought me a trophy that said, "Congratulations on Adulting." Remember, cupcakes are for adults too—treat yo' self!

INGREDIENTS

Chocolate Cupcake Batter
(see page 38)

Big Fish Buttercream
(see page 28)

½ cup (116 g) The Perfect
Puree Raspberry Puree

Preheat the oven to 325°F on convection mode or 350°F in a conventional oven. Line three cupcake pans with paper liners.

Prepare the batter, transfer it to a piping bag, and pipe it into the paper liners. Place the cupcakes in the oven and bake until their internal temperature is 200°F, 20 to 25 minutes, rotating the pans halfway through.

Remove the cupcakes from the oven and let them rest in the pans for 5 minutes. Using an offset spatula, remove the cupcakes from the pans and transfer them to a cupcake holder. Cover them tightly and let them cool completely.

When the cupcakes have cooled completely and are ready to be frosted, prepare the Big Fish Buttercream. With the mixer running, add the raspberry puree and beat until it has been incorporated.

Frost the cupcakes with the raspberry buttercream and serve.

Thai Tea Cupcakes

YIELD: 24 CUPCAKES / **ACTIVE TIME:** 20 MINUTES / **TOTAL TIME:** 50 MINUTES

One of my favorite drinks on a hot day is a Thai iced tea. Sweet, spicy, and creamy, I knew it was a flavor that would take to baking well. Tip: the more time these have to rest, the more intense the flavor gets. I suggest making them the day before you plan to enjoy them.

INGREDIENTS

2 cups (488 g) milk

¼ cup (76 g) condensed milk

¾ cup (60 g) Thai tea mix

1 cup (226 g) unsalted butter, softened

1¾ cups (350 g) sugar

4 (220 g) eggs

1 tablespoon (12 g) vanilla paste

2¾ cups (376 g) cake flour

2½ teaspoons (11.5 g) baking powder

¾ teaspoon (4 g) kosher salt

Big Fish Buttercream
(see page 28)

Preheat the oven to 325°F on convection mode or 350°F in a conventional oven. Line two cupcake pans with paper liners.

To begin preparations for the cupcakes, place the milks in a small saucepan and warm them to 180°F. Remove the pan from heat, add the tea, cover the pan, and let the mixture steep for 15 minutes. Strain and let the Thai tea milk cool.

Place the butter, sugar, and eggs in the work bowl of a stand mixer fitted with the paddle attachment and beat until the mixture is light and fluffy, 3 to 5 minutes. Add the vanilla and beat to incorporate.

Place the flour, baking powder, and salt in a bowl and whisk to combine. Sift the mixture through a fine-mesh tamis onto a piece of parchment paper. Fold the parchment paper lengthwise and alternate between adding small increments of the dry mixture and Thai tea milk to the work bowl, folding to incorporate each addition and scraping down the work bowl as needed.

Transfer the batter to a piping bag, pipe it into the paper liners, and place the cupcakes in the oven. Bake until their internal temperature is 200°F, 20 to 25 minutes, rotating the pans halfway through.

Remove the cupcakes from the oven and let them rest in the pans for 5 minutes. Using an offset spatula, remove the cupcakes from the pans and transfer them to a cupcake holder. Cover them tightly and let them cool completely.

When the cupcakes have cooled completely and are ready to be frosted, prepare the buttercream.

Frost the cupcakes with the buttercream and serve.

Engagement Cupcakes

YIELD: 24 CUPCAKES / **ACTIVE TIME:** 20 MINUTES / **TOTAL TIME:** 50 MINUTES

Celebrate the blooming love of your engagement with these adorable cupcakes. The flavor and texture of the red velvet batter are sure to symbolize the depth and richness of your bond. Cheers to your love story and the exciting moments yet to unfold. One thing: the buttercream will briefly split once the strawberry puree has been added; just keep on mixing until the buttercream has emulsified.

INGREDIENTS

Red velvet cupcake batter (see page 57)

Italian Meringue Buttercream (see page 29)

⅔ cup (150 g) The Perfect Puree Strawberry Puree

Preheat the oven to 325°F on convection mode or 350°F in a conventional oven. Line two cupcake pans with paper liners.

Prepare the batter, transfer it to a piping bag, and pipe it into the paper liners. Place the cupcakes in the oven and bake until their internal temperature is 200°F, 20 to 25 minutes, rotating the pans halfway through.

Remove the cupcakes from the oven and let them rest in the pans for 5 minutes. Using an offset spatula, remove the cupcakes from the pans and transfer them to a cupcake holder. Cover them tightly and let them cool completely.

When the cupcakes have cooled completely and are ready to be frosted, prepare the Italian Meringue Buttercream. With the mixer running, add the strawberry puree and beat until it has been incorporated, 1 to 2 minutes.

Frost the cupcakes with the buttercream and serve.

INGREDIENTS

FOR THE CUPCAKES

2⅔ cups (625 ml) heavy cream

½ cup (15 g) loose-leaf Earl Grey tea

2⅔ cups (538 g) sugar

6 (330 g) eggs

1 tablespoon (13 g) vanilla paste

4¾ cups (600 g) all-purpose flour

3¼ teaspoons (15 g) baking powder

½ teaspoon (3 g) kosher salt

FOR THE FILLING

¾ sheet (1.75 g) of silver gelatin

2 (110 g) eggs

½ cup (108 ml) fresh lemon juice

½ cup (108 g) sugar

⅔ cup (140 g) unsalted butter, softened

1 tablespoon (6 g) lemon zest

1 teaspoon (4 g) vanilla paste

Big Fish Buttercream
(see page 28)

Baby Shower Cupcakes

YIELD: 24 CUPCAKES / **ACTIVE TIME:** 20 MINUTES / **TOTAL TIME:** 55 MINUTES

I have been seeing a lot of neutral-toned baby showers, and these cupcakes are perfect for such an occasion, understated but delicate enough to give off those newborn vibes.

Preheat the oven to 325°F on convection mode or 350°F in a conventional oven. Line two cupcake pans with paper liners.

To begin preparations for the cupcakes, place the cream in a small saucepan and warm it to 180°F. Remove the pan from heat, add the tea, cover the pan, and let the mixture steep for 15 minutes. Strain and let the Earl Grey milk cool.

Place the sugar and eggs in the work bowl of a stand mixer fitted with the whisk attachment and whip on high until the mixture is light and fluffy, about 6 minutes. Add the vanilla and whip to incorporate.

Place the flour, baking powder, and salt in a bowl and whisk to combine. Sift the mixture through a fine-mesh tamis onto a piece of parchment paper. Fold the parchment paper lengthwise and alternate between adding small increments of the dry mixture and Earl Grey milk to the work bowl, folding to incorporate each addition and scraping down the work bowl as needed.

Transfer the batter to a piping bag, pipe it into the paper liners, and place the cupcakes in the oven. Bake until their internal temperature is 200°F, 20 to 25 minutes, rotating the pans halfway through.

Remove the cupcakes from the oven and let them rest in the pans for 5 minutes. Using an offset spatula, remove the cupcakes from the pans and transfer them to a cupcake holder. Cover them tightly and let them cool completely.

To begin preparations for the filling, submerge the gelatin sheet in cold water and let it bloom for 6 minutes. Place the eggs, lemon juice, and sugar in a small saucepan and warm the mixture over medium heat, whisking continually, until it is 140°F.

Transfer the mixture to a blender, add the bloomed gelatin, pinches of the butter, lemon zest, and vanilla and puree until the mixture is smooth and creamy. Transfer the curd to a bowl and place plastic wrap directly on the surface to prevent a skin from forming. Let the curd cool.

When the cupcakes have cooled completely and are ready to be frosted, prepare the buttercream.

Working from the tops of the cupcakes, remove their centers and fill them with the lemon curd. Frost the cupcakes with the buttercream and serve.

Pupcakes

YIELD: 12 CUPCAKES / **ACTIVE TIME:** 20 MINUTES / **TOTAL TIME:** 45 MINUTES

Stubborn, clown-like, bat-eared couch potatoes, Louie and Sunnie are typically pretty picky when it comes to treats. But, despite not liking being on set and having their photo taken, these pupcakes proved impossible to resist.

If you can't find oat flour, just pulse some raw oats in a food processor. I used two flavors of buttercream here, but customize to your pooch! A scoop of yogurt, drizzle of honey, plain peanut butter, whatever you (and they) are comfortable with!

INGREDIENTS

2 cups (240 g) oat flour

2 teaspoons (9 g) baking powder

2 teaspoons (5 g) Spice Girl Mix (see page 254)

½ teaspoon (2 g) baking soda

2 (110 g) eggs

½ cup (170 g) honey

2 cups (452 g) pumpkin puree

3 (300 g) bananas, peeled and mashed

Big Fish Buttercream (see page 28), with creamy peanut butter replacing half of the unsalted butter

Honey buttercream (see page 49)

12 Milk-Bones, for topping

Preheat the oven to 325°F on convection mode or 350°F in a conventional oven. Line a cupcake pan with paper liners.

Place all of the ingredients, except for the buttercreams and Milk-Bones, in the work bowl of a stand mixer fitted with the paddle attachment and beat until the mixture just comes together as a smooth batter.

Scoop the batter into the paper liners, place the cupcakes in the oven, and bake until their internal temperature is 200°F, 20 to 25 minutes, rotating the pan halfway through.

Remove the cupcakes from the oven and let them rest in the pan for 5 minutes. Using an offset spatula, remove the cupcakes from the pan and transfer them to a cupcake holder. Cover them tightly and let them cool completely.

When the cupcakes have cooled completely and are ready to be frosted, prepare the buttercreams.

Frost the cupcakes with the peanut butter buttercream and honey buttercream, top with the Milk-Bones, and let your pups have at them.

INGREDIENTS

FOR THE CUPCAKES

2 cups (400 g) sugar

1 cup (227 g) unsalted butter, softened

4 (440 g) eggs

1 teaspoon (4 g) vanilla paste

3 cups (375 g) all-purpose flour, plus more as needed

1 tablespoon (13 g) baking powder

½ teaspoon (3 g) kosher salt

1 cup (238 ml) buttermilk

Zest and juice of 4 lemons

1 cup (190 g) blueberries

FOR THE BUTTERCREAM

1 cup (226 g) unsalted butter, softened

3 cups (360 g) confectioners' sugar

1 teaspoon (4 g) vanilla paste

Zest and juice of 1 lemon

Lemon & Blueberry Cupcakes

YIELD: 24 CUPCAKES / **ACTIVE TIME:** 20 MINUTES / **TOTAL TIME:** 45 MINUTES

These bring a bright, refreshing touch to any occasion, especially a summer wedding. Tossing the blueberries in a bit of flour before adding them to the batter prevents them from sinking to the bottoms of the cupcakes while they are in the oven.

Preheat the oven to 325°F on convection mode or 350°F in a conventional oven. Line two cupcake pans with paper liners.

To begin preparations for the cupcakes, place the sugar and butter in the work bowl of a stand mixer fitted with the paddle attachment and cream until the mixture is light and fluffy, 3 to 5 minutes. Scrape down the work bowl, add the eggs one at a time, and beat to incorporate. Add the vanilla and whip to incorporate.

Place the flour, baking powder, and salt in a bowl and whisk to combine. Sift the mixture through a fine-mesh tamis onto a piece of parchment paper. Fold the parchment paper lengthwise and alternate between adding small increments of the dry mixture and buttermilk to the work bowl, beating to incorporate each addition and scraping down the work bowl as needed.

Add the lemon zest and lemon juice and beat to incorporate. Place the blueberries in a bowl, sprinkle a little flour over them, and toss to coat. Add the blueberries to the batter and fold until they are evenly distributed.

Transfer the batter to a piping bag, pipe it into the paper liners, and place the cupcakes in the oven. Bake until their internal temperature is 200°F, 20 to 25 minutes, rotating the pans halfway through.

Remove the cupcakes from the oven and let them rest in the pans for 5 minutes. Using an offset spatula, remove the cupcakes from the pans and transfer them to a cupcake holder. Cover them tightly and let them cool completely.

When the cupcakes have cooled completely and are ready to be frosted, prepare the buttercream. Place the butter in the work bowl of a stand mixer fitted with the paddle attachment and beat until it is light and fluffy, 3 to 5 minutes. Scrape down the work bowl, sift the confectioners' sugar into it, and beat until the mixture is smooth, light, and fluffy, about 3 minutes. Scrape down the work bowl, add the vanilla paste, lemon zest, and lemon juice, and beat until just incorporated.

Frost the cupcakes with the lemon buttercream and serve.

Red Velvet Cupcakes

YIELD: 24 CUPCAKES / **ACTIVE TIME:** 20 MINUTES / **TOTAL TIME:** 45 MINUTES

Red velvet cupcakes are just inevitable for every wedding baker out there. But the way you choose to decorate them can help your version stand out, as shown by this print design, which was inspired by a Brooklyn couple who bonded over their love of street art. As this particular design shows, adding cupcakes to your wedding desserts is an incredible avenue to create something unique that is based entirely around you and your partner.

INGREDIENTS

Red velvet cupcake batter
(see page 57)

Cream cheese buttercream
(see page 57)

Preheat the oven to 325°F on convection mode or 350°F in a conventional oven. Line two cupcake pans with paper liners.

Prepare the batter, transfer it to a piping bag, and pipe it into the paper liners. Place the cupcakes in the oven and bake until their internal temperature is 200°F, 20 to 25 minutes, rotating the pans halfway through.

Remove the cupcakes from the oven and let them rest in the pans for 5 minutes. Using an offset spatula, remove the cupcakes from the pans and transfer them to a cupcake holder. Cover them tightly and let them cool completely.

When the cupcakes have cooled completely and are ready to be frosted, prepare the buttercream.

Frost the cupcakes with the cream cheese buttercream and serve.

BIG FISH CLASSICS

This chapter collects those recipes that have proven to be the cornerstones of my business, Big Fish Cake Studio. Some are smash hits with the customers. Others are cupcakes that are personal favorites. All are sure to be beloved by whomever you prepare them for.

Whenevah Cupcakes

YIELD: 24 CUPCAKES / **ACTIVE TIME:** 20 MINUTES / **TOTAL TIME:** 50 MINUTES

Or "whenever" in "Downeast" slang. This cupcake is Big Fish's ode to Maine, and has been a standing favorite with both folks visiting from out of state, and all the Mainahs out heah, all year-round, for any occasion. For those who can't admit their love for cupcakes: this has blueberry pancake vibes.

Preheat the oven to 325°F on convection mode or 350°F for a conventional oven. Line two cupcake pans with paper liners.

To begin preparations for the cupcakes, place the butter, Crisco, maple syrup, sugar, and brown sugar in the work bowl of a stand mixer fitted with the paddle attachment and cream until the mixture is pale and fluffy, about 5 minutes. Scrape down the work bowl, add the eggs one at a time, and beat to incorporate. With the mixer running, add the canola oil in a slow stream.

Place the flour and baking powder in a bowl and whisk to combine. Sift the mixture through a fine-mesh tamis onto a piece of parchment paper. Fold the parchment paper lengthwise and alternate between adding small increments of the dry mixture, milk, and maple extract to the work bowl, beating to incorporate each addition and scraping down the work bowl as needed.

Transfer the batter to a piping bag, pipe it into the paper liners, and place the cupcakes in the oven. Bake until their internal temperature is 200°F, 20 to 25 minutes, rotating the pans halfway through.

Remove the cupcakes from the oven and let them rest in the pans for 5 minutes. Using an offset spatula, remove the cupcakes from the pans and transfer them to a cupcake holder. Cover them tightly and let them cool completely.

When the cupcakes have cooled completely and are ready to be frosted, prepare the buttercream. Place the maple syrup in a small saucepan and cook it over medium heat until it reaches 240°F. Place the eggs in the work bowl of a stand mixer fitted with the whisk attachment and whip them on high. With the mixer running at medium, add the hot maple syrup in a slow stream. Add the vanilla and salt and whip the mixture on high until it has doubled in volume and is pale and fluffy. Set the mixer to medium-low and add the butter in pinches. When all of the butter has been added, whip the buttercream on high until the butter has completely emulsified.

Frost the cupcakes with the maple buttercream, top them with the compote and Streusel, and serve.

INGREDIENTS

FOR THE CUPCAKES

5¾ tablespoons (82.5 g) unsalted butter, softened

⅓ cup (75 g) Crisco

⅓ cup (107 g) maple syrup

1⅔ cups (318.5 g) sugar

¼ cup (56 g) brown sugar

4 (220 g) eggs

⅓ cup (75 ml) canola oil

2⅓ cups (315 g) cake flour

1⅔ teaspoons (7.5 g) baking powder

½ cup (135 ml) whole milk

¼ cup (56 ml) maple extract

FOR THE BUTTERCREAM

1 (scant) cup (187 g) maple syrup

3 (165 g) eggs

1¾ teaspoons (8 g) vanilla paste

Pinch of kosher salt

3¼ cups (750 g) unsalted butter, softened

Blueberry Compote (see page 254), for topping

Streusel (see page 254), for topping

Mark Anthony Cupcakes

YIELD: 36 CUPCAKES / **ACTIVE TIME:** 20 MINUTES / **TOTAL TIME:** 50 MINUTES

We all know that cake and coffee go hand in hand. Add a touch of chocolate, a splash of bourbon, and you cannot go wrong. That's why it's a classic in our studio. The name was inspired by one of our own big fish— it has just enough attitude, is a touch more masculine, and is a little bit bitter, but at the end of the day, it's a cupcake.

INGREDIENTS

FOR THE CUPCAKES

Vanilla Cupcake Batter
(see page 34)

¼ cup (52 ml) Trablit Coffee Extract

Milk Chocolate Ganache
(see page 255), for filling

FOR THE BUTTERCREAM

Big Fish Buttercream
(see page 28)

3 tablespoons (39 ml) Trablit Coffee Extract

Preheat the oven to 325°F on convection mode or 350°F for a conventional oven. Line three cupcake pans with paper liners.

To begin preparations for the cupcakes, prepare the batter and place half of it in a separate bowl. Add the coffee extract to one portion and stir to incorporate it. Transfer the espresso batter and the vanilla batter to their own piping bags and pipe the batters into the paper liners, swirling them.

Place the cupcakes in the oven and bake until their internal temperature is 200°F, 20 to 25 minutes, rotating the pans halfway through.

Remove the cupcakes from the oven and let them rest in the pans for 5 minutes. Using an offset spatula, remove the cupcakes from the pans and transfer them to a cupcake holder. Cover them tightly and let them cool completely.

When the cupcakes have cooled completely and are ready to be frosted, prepare the Big Fish Buttercream. With the mixer running, add the coffee extract and beat until it has been incorporated.

Working from the tops of the cupcakes, remove their centers and fill them with the ganache. Frost the cupcakes with the espresso buttercream and serve.

Coachella Cupcakes

YIELD: 36 CUPCAKES / **ACTIVE TIME:** 20 MINUTES / **TOTAL TIME:** 50 MINUTES

Passion fruit has the intense tartness of citrus and pairs perfectly with baked goods. Coconut? Soft and light. White chocolate? Sweet, yet rich. This recipe is one of my personal favorites, but, surprisingly, our least-ordered cupcake. Still, I refuse to remove it from my classics menu, and hope that putting it in this book will open people's eyes.

INGREDIENTS

Coconut cupcake batter (see page 61)

½ cup (132 g) passion fruit puree

2⅔ cups (346 g) chopped white chocolate

¼ cup (66 ml) heavy cream

2 tablespoons (46 g) glucose

1⅓ tablespoons (20 g) unsalted butter, softened

White chocolate buttercream (see page 42)

Unsweetened coconut flakes, toasted, for topping

Preheat the oven to 325°F on convection mode or 350°F for a conventional oven. Line three cupcake pans with paper liners.

Prepare the batter, transfer it to a piping bag, and pipe it into the paper liners. Place the cupcakes in the oven and bake until their internal temperature is 200°F, 20 to 25 minutes, rotating the pans halfway through.

Remove the cupcakes from the oven and let them rest in the pans for 5 minutes. Using an offset spatula, remove the cupcakes from the pans and transfer them to a cupcake holder. Cover them tightly and let them cool completely.

Place the passion fruit puree in a small saucepan and bring it to a simmer over medium heat. Cook until the puree has reduced by half, about 10 minutes.

Place the white chocolate in a bowl and pour the reduced passion fruit puree over it.

Place the heavy cream and glucose in a medium saucepan and bring to a boil. Add the chocolate mixture, cook for 30 seconds, and then stir with a rubber spatula until the mixture is smooth.

Add the butter and stir until it has melted. Remove the pan from heat and let the ganache cool until it is firm enough to pipe or quenelle.

When the cupcakes have cooled completely and are ready to be frosted, prepare the buttercream.

Frost the cupcakes with the white chocolate buttercream, top them with the passion fruit ganache and toasted coconut, and serve.

Bona Fide Cupcakes

YIELD: 36 CUPCAKES / **ACTIVE TIME:** 20 MINUTES / **TOTAL TIME:** 50 MINUTES

For chocolate lovers, these are the real deal. Full-on, souped-up, top-shelf—however you like to soothe your chocolate cravings, these will hit the mark.

INGREDIENTS

Chocolate Cupcake Batter
(see page 38)

Big Fish Buttercream
(see page 28)

½ lb. (226 g) dark chocolate,
melted and cooled to 90°F

Milk Chocolate Ganache
(see page 255), for filling

Cacao Nib Crumb (see page
254), for topping

Preheat the oven to 325°F on convection mode or 350°F for a conventional oven. Line three cupcake pans with paper liners.

Prepare the batter, transfer it to a piping bag, and pipe it into the paper liners. Place the cupcakes in the oven and bake until their internal temperature is 200°F, 20 to 25 minutes, rotating the pans halfway through.

Remove the cupcakes from the oven and let them rest in the pans for 5 minutes. Using an offset spatula, remove the cupcakes from the pans and transfer them to a cupcake holder. Cover them tightly and let them cool completely.

When the cupcakes have cooled completely and are ready to be frosted, prepare the Big Fish Buttercream. Add the melted chocolate and beat until it is incorporated.

Working from the bottoms of the cupcakes, remove their centers and fill them with the ganache. Frost the cupcakes with the dark chocolate buttercream, sprinkle some of the Cacao Nib Crumb over the top, and serve.

BONA FIDE CUPCAKES, SEE PAGE 87

Heiress Cupcakes

YIELD: 36 CUPCAKES / **ACTIVE TIME:** 20 MINUTES / **TOTAL TIME:** 50 MINUTES

These cupcakes are whimsical and mysterious, bridal meets fairy tale meets tea party. The most popular flavor at Big Fish, year after year.

INGREDIENTS

Earl Grey cupcake batter
(see page 73)

Honey buttercream
(see page 49)

Mixed Berry Compote
(see page 255), for topping

Preheat the oven to 325°F on convection mode or 350°F for a conventional oven. Line three cupcake pans with paper liners.

Prepare the batter, transfer it to a piping bag, and pipe it into the paper liners. Place the cupcakes in the oven and bake until their internal temperature is 200°F, 20 to 25 minutes, rotating the pans halfway through.

Remove the cupcakes from the oven and let them rest in the pans for 5 minutes. Using an offset spatula, remove the cupcakes from the pans and transfer them to a cupcake holder. Cover them tightly and let them cool completely.

When the cupcakes have cooled completely and are ready to be frosted, prepare the buttercream.

Frost the cupcakes with the honey buttercream, top them with the compote, and serve.

MODERN TWISTS ON TRADITION

*B*eing classically trained in the pastry arts means mastering the foundational recipes, those confections that have been admired and beloved for centuries. And while my own path has led me away from a place where I would be making them night after night, many of them do remain front of mind and close to my heart, a combination that frequently brings to mind new ways to make use of the greatness that has carried them for so long. This chapter collects the cupcakes that are some of my best takes on those desserts we all know and love, proof that part of being considered classic in the culinary world is leaving space for innovation.

Cannoli Cupcakes

YIELD: 36 CUPCAKES / **ACTIVE TIME:** 20 MINUTES / **TOTAL TIME:** 50 MINUTES

As you would expect, these are rich yet light, comforting while at the same time a guilty pleasure.

INGREDIENTS

FOR THE CUPCAKES

White Cupcake Batter
(see page 35)

1½ teaspoons (3 g)
cardamom

FOR THE TOPPING

¼ cup (50 g) roasted
pistachios

2 tablespoons (16 g)
chopped chocolate

2 tablespoons (23 g) cacao
nibs

¼ teaspoon (1.5 g) fine sea
salt

FOR THE
BUTTERCREAM

Big Fish Buttercream
(see page 28)

2 cups (454 g) ricotta cheese

Zest of 1 orange

Pinch of cardamom

Preheat the oven to 325°F on convection mode or 350°F for a conventional oven. Line three cupcake pans with paper liners.

To begin preparations for the cupcakes, prepare the batter, adding the cardamom along with the other dry ingredients. Transfer the batter to a piping bag and pipe it into the paper liners. Place the cupcakes in the oven and bake until their internal temperature is 200°F, 20 to 25 minutes, rotating the pans halfway through.

Remove the cupcakes from the oven and let them rest in the pans for 5 minutes. Using an offset spatula, remove the cupcakes from the pans and transfer them to a cupcake holder. Cover them tightly and let them cool completely.

To prepare the topping, place all of the ingredients in a food processor and pulse until they are finely ground.

When the cupcakes have cooled completely and are ready to be frosted, prepare the Big Fish Buttercream. Add the ricotta, orange zest, and cardamom and fold to incorporate.

Frost the cupcakes with the buttercream, sprinkle the topping over them, and serve.

Matcha Cupcakes

YIELD: 24 CUPCAKES / **ACTIVE TIME:** 20 MINUTES / **TOTAL TIME:** 50 MINUTES

While quality matcha should have a sweet finish, it is best known for its earthy undertones. Most people who do love it do not enjoy overly sweet desserts, which is why matcha is a perfect match for my baking style.

INGREDIENTS

FOR THE CUPCAKES

Earl Grey cupcake batter (see page 73), with ½ cup (108 g) matcha powder replacing the loose-leaf Earl Grey tea

FOR THE BUTTERCREAM

Big Fish Buttercream (see page 28)

2 tablespoons (27 g) matcha powder

¾ cup (105 g) melted white chocolate (28 percent), cooled to 90°F

Preheat the oven to 325°F on convection mode or 350°F for a conventional oven. Line two cupcake pans with paper liners.

To begin preparations for the cupcakes, prepare the batter, transfer it to a piping bag, and pipe it into the paper liners. Place the cupcakes in the oven and bake until their internal temperature is 200°F, 20 to 25 minutes, rotating the pans halfway through.

Remove the cupcakes from the oven and let them rest in the pans for 5 minutes. Using an offset spatula, remove the cupcakes from the pans and transfer them to a cupcake holder. Cover them tightly and let them cool completely.

When the cupcakes have cooled completely and are ready to be frosted, prepare the Big Fish Buttercream. Add the matcha powder and beat to incorporate. Add the white chocolate and beat until it is emulsified.

Frost the cupcakes with the matcha buttercream and serve.

Bananas Foster Cupcakes

YIELD: 36 CUPCAKES / **ACTIVE TIME:** 20 MINUTES / **TOTAL TIME:** 50 MINUTES

I'm not going to lie, I tried to flambé these cupcakes in the studio, and it did not go well. I opted for brûléed banana slices, which results in a more refined cupcake that still highlights the caramelized character of this delicacy.

INGREDIENTS

FOR THE CUPCAKES

8 (907 g) ripe bananas, peeled

½ cup (113 ml) heavy cream

½ cup (115 g) crème fraîche

2⅛ cups (454 g) sugar

4 (220 g) eggs

½ cup (113 ml) canola oil

2 tablespoons (26 ml) LorAnn Butter Rum oil

4⅓ cups (538 g) all-purpose flour

1¾ tablespoons (24 g) baking powder

FOR THE BUTTERCREAM

Big Fish Buttercream (see page 28)

½ cup (113 g) Fabbri Caramel Delipaste

Preheat the oven to 325°F on convection mode or 350°F in a conventional oven. Line three cupcake pans with paper liners.

To begin preparations for the cupcakes, place the bananas, heavy cream, and crème fraîche in the work bowl of a stand mixer fitted with the paddle attachment and beat until the mixture is combined, 1 to 2 minutes. Add the sugar and beat for 1 minute. Add the eggs and oils and beat to incorporate.

Place the flour and baking powder in a bowl and whisk to combine. Sift the mixture through a fine-mesh tamis onto a piece of parchment paper. Fold the parchment paper lengthwise and add small increments of the dry mixture into the work bowl, beating to incorporate each addition and scraping down the work bowl as needed.

Transfer the batter to a piping bag, pipe it into the paper liners, and place the cupcakes in the oven. Bake until their internal temperature is 200°F, 20 to 25 minutes, rotating the pans halfway through.

Remove the cupcakes from the oven and let them rest in the pans for 5 minutes. Using an offset spatula, remove the cupcakes from the pans and transfer them to a cupcake holder. Cover them tightly and let them cool completely.

When the cupcakes have cooled completely and are ready to be frosted, prepare the Big Fish Buttercream. Add the caramel paste and beat until it has emulsified.

Frost the cupcakes with the caramel buttercream and serve.

Crème Brûlée Cupcakes

YIELD: 36 CUPCAKES / **ACTIVE TIME:** 20 MINUTES / **TOTAL TIME:** 50 MINUTES

The season I translated this flavor into cake form, it was by far the most popular flavor for weddings. Most of my clients are big dessert lovers, so when we interpret a classic dessert, it tends to result in a winner. Fun fact: I learned the technique of brûlée from Dieter Schorner, the man who brought crème brûlée to the United States. He was a professor of mine in culinary school, and I will never forget the moment when he wrapped his hands around mine on the blowtorch and taught me his technique.

INGREDIENTS

Vanilla Cupcake Batter (see page 34)

½ cup (100 g) isomalt

Caramel buttercream (see page 98)

Dulce de Leche (see page 255), for filling

Pastry Cream (see page 256), for filling

Preheat the oven to 325°F on convection mode or 350°F in a conventional oven. Line three cupcake pans with paper liners.

Prepare the batter, transfer it to a piping bag, and pipe it into the paper liners. Place the cupcakes in the oven and bake until their internal temperature is 200°F, 20 to 25 minutes, rotating the pans halfway through.

Remove the cupcakes from the oven and let them rest in the pans for 5 minutes. Using an offset spatula, remove the cupcakes from the pans and transfer them to a cupcake holder. Cover them tightly and let them cool completely. Leave the oven on.

Line a rimmed baking sheet with a Silpat mat. Place the isomalt in a small saucepan and melt it over low heat, stirring continually with a rubber spatula. Put on two to three pairs of latex gloves. Pour the melted isomalt into the baking sheet, place it in the oven, and bake in 45-second intervals. Carefully remove the isomalt from the oven and pinch tuiles from it. This technique will take a little getting used to, but eventually you will get it. Just make sure you are careful and work fast, as isomalt has a very high melting point and retains a lot of heat.

When the cupcakes have cooled completely and are ready to be frosted, prepare the buttercream.

Working from the tops of the cupcakes, remove their centers and fill them with the Dulce de Leche and Pastry Cream. Frost the cupcakes with the caramel buttercream, top them with the tuiles, and serve.

CRÈME BRÛLÉE CUPCAKES, SEE PAGE 99

Boston Cream Cupcakes

YIELD: 36 CUPCAKES / **ACTIVE TIME:** 20 MINUTES / **TOTAL TIME:** 1 HOUR

First it was a pie. Then it was a doughnut. Now it's a cupcake. Who knows what's next for the beloved Boston cream.

INGREDIENTS

White Cupcake Batter
(see page 35)

Italian Meringue
Buttercream (see page 29)

Pastry Cream (see page 256),
for filling

Butter Ganache
(see page 255)

Preheat the oven to 325°F on convection mode or 350°F in a conventional oven. Line three cupcake pans with paper liners.

Prepare the batter, transfer it to a piping bag, and pipe it into the paper liners. Place the cupcakes in the oven and bake until their internal temperature is 200°F, 20 to 25 minutes, rotating the pans halfway through.

Remove the cupcakes from the oven and let them rest in the pans for 5 minutes. Using an offset spatula, remove the cupcakes from the pans and transfer them to a cupcake holder. Cover them tightly and let them cool completely.

When the cupcakes have cooled completely and are ready to be frosted, prepare the buttercream.

Working from the tops of the cupcakes, remove their centers and fill them with the Pastry Cream. Frost the cupcakes with the buttercream and refrigerate them for 10 minutes.

Dip the buttercream into the ganache, let it set for a few minutes, and serve.

Strawberry Shortcake Cupcakes

YIELD: 36 CUPCAKES / **ACTIVE TIME:** 20 MINUTES / **TOTAL TIME:** 50 MINUTES

Let's be honest—it's not the cake, it's not the strawberries, and it's not the cream that makes this dessert so beloved. Instead, it's the sweet juice created by macerating the strawberries, which is a powerful enough variable to separate a good version from a lacking one.

INGREDIENTS

White Cupcake Batter
(see page 35)

Chantilly (see page 256),
for topping

Macerated Strawberries
(see page 256), for topping

Preheat the oven to 325°F on convection mode or 350°F in a conventional oven. Line three cupcake pans with paper liners.

Prepare the batter, transfer it to a piping bag, and pipe it into the paper liners. Place the cupcakes in the oven and bake until their internal temperature is 200°F, 20 to 25 minutes, rotating the pans halfway through.

Remove the cupcakes from the oven and let them rest in the pans for 5 minutes. Using an offset spatula, remove the cupcakes from the pans and transfer them to a cupcake holder. Cover them tightly and let them cool completely.

Top the cupcakes with the Chantilly and Macerated Strawberries and serve.

Lemon Meringue Cupcakes

YIELD: 36 CUPCAKES / **ACTIVE TIME:** 20 MINUTES / **TOTAL TIME:** 50 MINUTES

My grandpa loved pie so much that he wasn't fully on board when I told him I was starting a cake business. I think he would be more than OK with these cupcakes, though. Here's to the original Big Fish.

INGREDIENTS

Butter Cupcake Batter
(see page 36)

Zest of 3 lemons

Lemon curd (see page 73),
for filling

Graham Cracker Crumb
(see page 256), for filling

Meringue (see page 257,
for topping

Preheat the oven to 325°F on convection mode or 350°F for a conventional oven. Line three cupcake pans with paper liners.

Prepare the batter, adding the lemon zest toward the end of the mixing process. Transfer it to a piping bag and pipe the batter into the paper liners.

Place the cupcakes in the oven and bake until their internal temperature is 200°F, 20 to 25 minutes, rotating the pans halfway through.

Remove the cupcakes from the oven and let them rest in the pans for 5 minutes. Using an offset spatula, remove the cupcakes from the pans and transfer them to a cupcake holder. Cover them tightly and let them cool completely.

Working from the tops of the cupcakes, remove their centers and fill them with the lemon curd and Graham Cracker Crumb. Spread the Meringue over the top of the cupcakes, toast it with a kitchen torch, and serve.

Tiramisu Cupcakes

YIELD: 36 CUPCAKES / **ACTIVE TIME:** 20 MINUTES / **TOTAL TIME:** 50 MINUTES

The generous dusting of cocoa powder on top adds the finishing touch, capturing the essence of traditional tiramisu in every bite.

INGREDIENTS

Espresso cupcake batter
(see page 85)

1 cup (227 g) unsalted butter,
softened

2½ cups (300 g)
confectioners' sugar

¾ cup (180 g) mascarpone
cheese

1 teaspoon (4 g) vanilla paste

Milk Chocolate Ganache
(see page 255), with Kahlúa
replacing the bourbon,
for filling

Cocoa powder, for topping

Preheat the oven to 325°F on convection mode or 350°F for a conventional oven. Line three cupcake pans with paper liners.

Prepare the batter, transfer it to a piping bag, and pipe the batter into the paper liners.

Place the cupcakes in the oven and bake until their internal temperature is 200°F, 20 to 25 minutes, rotating the pans halfway through.

Remove the cupcakes from the oven and let them rest in the pans for 5 minutes. Using an offset spatula, remove the cupcakes from the pans and transfer them to a cupcake holder. Cover them tightly and let them cool completely.

Place the butter and confectioners' sugar in the work bowl of a stand mixer fitted with the paddle attachment and beat until the mixture is light and fluffy, 3 to 5 minutes. Scrape down the work bowl, add the mascarpone and vanilla, and beat on medium until just incorporated.

Working from the tops of the cupcakes, remove their centers and fill them with the ganache. Frost the cupcakes with the mascarpone buttercream, sprinkle some cocoa powder over them, and serve.

Coffee Cake Cupcakes

YIELD: 36 CUPCAKES / **ACTIVE TIME:** 20 MINUTES / **TOTAL TIME:** 50 MINUTES

Bring these to brunch! Super quick and easier than baking a whole coffee cake. And definitely easier than being in charge of the hollandaise.

INGREDIENTS

Butter Cupcake Batter
(see page 36)

2 tablespoons (14 g) Spice
Girl Mix (see page 254)

Streusel (see page 254),
for topping

Sour Cream Glaze (see page
257), for topping

Preheat the oven to 325°F on convection mode or 350°F for a conventional oven. Line three cupcake pans with paper liners.

Prepare the batter, adding the Spice Girl Mix along with the other dry ingredients. Transfer it to a piping bag and pipe the batter into the paper liners.

Place the cupcakes in the oven and bake until their internal temperature is 200°F, 20 to 25 minutes, rotating the pans halfway through.

Remove the cupcakes from the oven and let them rest in the pans for 5 minutes. Using an offset spatula, remove the cupcakes from the pans and transfer them to a cupcake holder. Cover them tightly and let them cool completely.

Top the cupcakes with the Streusel and Sour Cream Glaze and serve.

German Chocolate Cupcakes

YIELD: 36 CUPCAKES / **ACTIVE TIME:** 20 MINUTES / **TOTAL TIME:** 50 MINUTES

I just skipped the buttercream here and put the traditional filling right on top, a move that amplifies the very best part of what a German chocolate cake should be.

INGREDIENTS

Chocolate Cupcake Batter (see page 38)

½ cup (115 g) unsalted butter

1 cup (200 g) brown sugar

3 (54 g) egg yolks

1 (240 ml) can of evaporated milk

1 cup (125 g) pecans, chopped and roasted

2 cups (186 g) sweetened coconut flakes

1 teaspoon (4 g) vanilla paste

Preheat the oven to 325°F on convection mode or 350°F for a conventional oven. Line three cupcake pans with paper liners.

Prepare the batter, transfer it to a piping bag, and pipe the batter into the paper liners. Place the cupcakes in the oven and bake until their internal temperature is 200°F, 20 to 25 minutes, rotating the pans halfway through.

While the cupcakes are baking, place the butter, brown sugar, egg yolks, and evaporated milk in a medium saucepan and bring to a boil over medium heat, stirring continually, until the mixture has thickened, about 5 minutes. Remove the pan from heat and stir in the pecans, coconut, and vanilla. Let the mixture cool to room temperature.

Remove the cupcakes from the oven and let them rest in the pans for 5 minutes. Using an offset spatula, remove the cupcakes from the pans and transfer them to a cupcake holder. Cover them tightly and let them cool completely.

Top the cupcakes with the coconut-and-pecan mixture and serve.

S'mores Cupcakes

YIELD: 36 CUPCAKES / **ACTIVE TIME:** 20 MINUTES / **TOTAL TIME:** 50 MINUTES

For me, the best part of a s'more is the fire. To give these that flavor, I like to smoke my egg whites before whipping them into a meringue. To do this, use a kitchen smoking gun and simply cover a container of whites with aluminum foil. Slip the smoking tube under the foil so the smoke won't leak out. Once you've filled the container with smoke, tightly cover the egg whites and let the smoke infuse for at least 30 minutes before whipping.

INGREDIENTS

Chocolate Cupcake Batter
(see page 38)

Meringue (see page 257),
for topping

Graham Cracker Crumb
(see page 256), for topping

Milk Chocolate Ganache
(see page 255), for topping

Preheat the oven to 325°F on convection mode or 350°F for a conventional oven. Line three cupcake pans with paper liners.

Prepare the batter, transfer it to a piping bag, and pipe the batter into the paper liners.

Place the cupcakes in the oven and bake until their internal temperature is 200°F, 20 to 25 minutes, rotating the pans halfway through.

Remove the cupcakes from the oven and let them rest in the pans for 5 minutes. Using an offset spatula, remove the cupcakes from the pans and transfer them to a cupcake holder. Cover them tightly and let them cool completely.

Spread the Meringue over the cupcakes, sprinkle some of the Graham Cracker Crumb over it, and toast it with a kitchen torch. Drizzle some ganache over the top and serve.

S'MORES CUPCAKES, SEE PAGE 113

Molten Chocolate Cupcakes

YIELD: 6 CUPCAKES / **ACTIVE TIME:** 20 MINUTES / **TOTAL TIME:** 30 MINUTES

A happy accident resulted in this great recipe for small dinner parties, since you can make them in advance, store them in the refrigerator, and pop them in the oven just before serving.

Dust with confectioners' sugar and fresh fruit or mint for a pop of color, chef's choice.

INGREDIENTS

½ cup (75 g) dark chocolate

½ cup (113 g) unsalted butter

1 (55 g) egg

1 (18 g) egg yolk

2 tablespoons (15 g) all-purpose flour

¼ cup (30 g) confectioners' sugar

Pinch of kosher salt

Preheat the oven to 350°F on convection mode or 375°F for a conventional oven. Generously coat a cupcake pan with nonstick cooking spray.

Fill a medium saucepan halfway with water and bring to a simmer. Place the chocolate and butter in a bain-marie or heatproof bowl, place it over the simmering water, and stir until the mixture is melted and smooth. Remove the container from heat and set it aside.

Place the egg and egg yolk in a mixing bowl and whisk to combine. Add the flour, confectioners' sugar, and salt and whisk to combine. Add the melted chocolate mixture and whisk until the resulting mixture just comes together as a smooth batter.

Transfer the batter to a piping bag and pipe it into the prepared cupcake pan. Place the cupcakes in the oven and bake for 7 minutes.

Remove the cupcakes from the oven and let them rest in the pan for 3 minutes. Place a large cutting board over the pan and carefully and quickly invert the pan; the cupcakes should pop right out. Serve immediately.

Key Lime Cupcakes

YIELD: 36 CUPCAKES / **ACTIVE TIME:** 20 MINUTES / **TOTAL TIME:** 50 MINUTES

If I am going to follow in my grandpa's footsteps and indulge in a piece of pie, it will be key lime, for sure.

INGREDIENTS

FOR THE CUPCAKES

White Cupcake Batter
(see page 35)

Zest of 2 key limes

FOR THE FILLING

¾ sheet (1.75 g) of silver gelatin

2 (110 g) eggs

½ cup (108 ml) fresh key lime juice

½ cup (108 g) sugar

⅔ cup (140 g) unsalted butter, softened

1 tablespoon (6 g) key lime zest

1 teaspoon (4 g) vanilla paste

Chantilly (see page 256), for topping

Graham Cracker Crumb (see page 256), for topping

Preheat the oven to 325°F on convection mode or 350°F for a conventional oven. Line three cupcake pans with paper liners.

To begin preparations for the cupcakes, prepare the batter, adding the key lime zest toward the end of the mixing process. Transfer it to a piping bag and pipe the batter into the paper liners.

Place the cupcakes in the oven and bake until their internal temperature is 200°F, 20 to 25 minutes, rotating the pans halfway through.

Remove the cupcakes from the oven and let them rest in the pans for 5 minutes. Using an offset spatula, remove the cupcakes from the pans and transfer them to a cupcake holder. Cover them tightly and let them cool completely.

To begin preparations for the filling, submerge the gelatin sheet in cold water and let it bloom for 6 minutes. Place the eggs, key lime juice, and sugar in a small saucepan and warm the mixture over medium heat, whisking continually, until it is 140°F.

Transfer the mixture to a blender, add the bloomed gelatin, pinches of the butter, key lime zest, and vanilla, and puree until the mixture is smooth and creamy. Transfer the curd to a bowl and place plastic wrap directly on the surface to prevent a skin from forming. Let the curd cool.

Working from the tops of the cupcakes, remove their centers and fill them with the key lime curd. Top the cupcakes with the Chantilly and Graham Cracker Crumb and serve.

KEY LIME CUPCAKES, SEE PAGE 117

Black Forest Cupcakes

YIELD: 36 CUPCAKES / **ACTIVE TIME:** 20 MINUTES / **TOTAL TIME:** 50 MINUTES

Luxardo cherries, although still very sweet, add a decadence to these cupcakes that helps produce one of my favorite flavor combinations in all of pastry making.

INGREDIENTS

Chocolate Cupcake Batter (see page 38)

Chantilly (see page 256), for topping

Luxardo cherries, for topping

Syrup from Luxardo Cherries, for topping

Dark chocolate shavings, for topping

Preheat the oven to 325°F on convection mode or 350°F for a conventional oven. Line three cupcake pans with paper liners.

Prepare the batter, transfer it to a piping bag, and pipe the batter into the paper liners.

Place the cupcakes in the oven and bake until their internal temperature is 200°F, 20 to 25 minutes, rotating the pans halfway through.

Remove the cupcakes from the oven and let them rest in the pans for 5 minutes. Using an offset spatula, remove the cupcakes from the pans and transfer them to a cupcake holder. Cover them tightly and let them cool completely.

Top the cupcakes with the Chantilly, cherries, syrup, and dark chocolate shavings and serve.

Triple Chocolate Cupcakes

YIELD: 36 CUPCAKES / **ACTIVE TIME:** 20 MINUTES / **TOTAL TIME:** 50 MINUTES

Don't just indulge your chocolate cravings, overwhelm them with these luscious cupcakes.

INGREDIENTS

Chocolate Cupcake Batter
(see page 38)

Dark chocolate buttercream
(see page 87)

White Chocolate Ganache
(see page 257), for filling

Chocolate candies,
for topping

White chocolate shavings,
for topping

Preheat the oven to 325°F on convection mode or 350°F for a conventional oven. Line three cupcake pans with paper liners.

Prepare the batter, transfer it to a piping bag, and pipe the batter into the paper liners. Place the cupcakes in the oven and bake until their internal temperature is 200°F, 20 to 25 minutes, rotating the pans halfway through.

Remove the cupcakes from the oven and let them rest in the pans for 5 minutes. Using an offset spatula, remove the cupcakes from the pans and transfer them to a cupcake holder. Cover them tightly and let them cool completely.

When the cupcakes have cooled completely and are ready to be frosted, prepare the buttercream.

Working from the tops of the cupcakes, remove their centers and fill them with the ganache. Frost them with the dark chocolate buttercream, sprinkle chocolate candies and white chocolate shavings over the top, and serve.

Sacher Cupcakes

YIELD: 30 CUPCAKES / **ACTIVE TIME:** 20 MINUTES / **TOTAL TIME:** 50 MINUTES

Based on the famous Sacher torte from Hotel Sacher in Vienna, Austria. The key notes are rich dark chocolate and apricot preserves, but I add a subtle note of hazelnut to help balance the sweetness of the apricot against the chocolate.

INGREDIENTS

FOR THE CUPCAKES

Chocolate Cupcake Batter (see page 38), with hazelnut flour replacing the all-purpose flour

Splash of Frangelico

FOR THE BUTTERCREAM

1¼ cups (250 g) sugar

4 (232 g) eggs

2 cups (454 g) unsalted butter, softened

1 cup (300 g) Nutella

Apricot Jam (see page 259), for topping

Preheat the oven to 325°F on convection mode or 350°F for a conventional oven. Line three cupcake pans with paper liners.

To begin preparations for the cupcakes, prepare the batter, adding the Frangelico toward the end of the mixing process. Transfer it to a piping bag and pipe the batter into the paper liners.

Place the cupcakes in the oven and bake until their internal temperature is 200°F, 20 to 25 minutes, rotating the pans halfway through.

Remove the cupcakes from the oven and let them rest in the pans for 5 minutes. Using an offset spatula, remove the cupcakes from the pans and transfer them to a cupcake holder. Cover them tightly and let them cool completely.

When the cupcakes have cooled completely and are ready to be frosted, prepare the buttercream. In a medium saucepan on medium heat, cook the sugar until it is 240°F. Place the eggs in the work bowl of a stand mixer fitted with the whisk attachment and whip on high. With the mixer running at medium, carefully stream the hot sugar into the eggs. Set the mixer back to high and whip until the mixture has cooled completely, about 10 minutes. Set the mixer to low, add the butter and Nutella, and whip until they are just emulsified.

Frost the cupcakes with the praline buttercream, top them with the Apricot Jam, and serve.

SPRING

Spring supplies needed energy after the long winter, and this burst cries out for impromptu celebrations and fresh, vibrant tasting treats that can match the exhilarating feeling of the world returning to life. Floral, bright, fruity, and beautiful, these cupcakes ensure that your spring celebrations will always come to a fitting close.

Ginger & Rose Cupcakes

YIELD: 36 CUPCAKES / **ACTIVE TIME:** 20 MINUTES / **TOTAL TIME:** 50 MINUTES

Spicy, sweet, and floral—think digestif in cupcake form when you're about to prepare these.

INGREDIENTS

White Cupcake Batter
(see page 35)

2 tablespoons (25 ml)
rose water

1½ teaspoons (9 g) ginger
paste

1 teaspoon (2 g) ground
ginger

Rose buttercream
(see page 60)

Preheat the oven to 325°F on convection mode or 350°F for a conventional oven. Line three cupcake pans with paper liners.

Prepare the batter, adding the rose water and ginger paste with the wet ingredients and the ground ginger with the dry ingredients.

Transfer the batter to a piping bag and pipe the batter into the paper liners. Place the cupcakes in the oven and bake until their internal temperature is 200°F, 20 to 25 minutes, rotating the pans halfway through.

Remove the cupcakes from the oven and let them rest in the pans for 5 minutes. Using an offset spatula, remove the cupcakes from the pans and transfer them to a cupcake holder. Cover them tightly and let them cool completely.

When the cupcakes have cooled completely and are ready to be frosted, prepare the buttercream.

Frost the cupcakes with the rose buttercream and serve.

Olive Oil Cupcakes

YIELD: 24 CUPCAKES / **ACTIVE TIME:** 25 MINUTES / **TOTAL TIME:** 50 MINUTES

Looking for a light, delicate dessert with enough versatility to serve throughout the day and seasons? This olive oil cake has a moist, tender crumb and can be paired with citrus, herbs, spices, and various creams for a more healthy cupcake. For spring, I garnished these with some edible dried florals.

INGREDIENTS

4 (210 g) eggs

1½ cups (300 g) sugar

1 cup (216 ml) extra-virgin olive oil

1 cup (245 g) yogurt

2 teaspoons (8 g) vanilla paste

2½ cups (312 g) all-purpose flour

2 teaspoons (9 g) baking powder

2 teaspoons (9 g) baking soda

Pinch of kosher salt

Mascarpone buttercream (see page 109)

Preheat the oven to 325°F on convection mode or 350°F for a conventional oven. Line two cupcake pans with paper liners.

Place the eggs, sugar, olive oil, yogurt, and vanilla in a mixing bowl and whisk to combine. Place the flour, baking powder, baking soda, and salt in a separate bowl and whisk to combine. Sift the dry mixture through a fine-mesh tamis onto a piece of parchment paper. Fold the parchment paper lengthwise, add the dry mixture to the wet mixture in small increments, and whisk to combine. Transfer the batter to a piping bag and pipe it into the paper liners.

Place the cupcakes in the oven and bake until their internal temperature is 200°F, 20 to 25 minutes, rotating the pans halfway through.

Remove the cupcakes from the oven and let them rest in the pans for 5 minutes. Using an offset spatula, remove the cupcakes from the pans and transfer them to a cupcake holder. Cover them tightly and let them cool completely.

When the cupcakes are completely cool and ready to be frosted, prepare the buttercream.

Frost the cupcakes with the mascarpone buttercream and serve.

Strawberry Rhubarb Cupcakes

YIELD: 36 CUPCAKES / **ACTIVE TIME:** 20 MINUTES / **TOTAL TIME:** 50 MINUTES

My grandma grows the most magnificent rhubarb on the block. When I was working in professional kitchens she would share about 10 pounds with me every few weeks to incorporate into my desserts. Although I can't touch her strawberry rhubarb pie, I do have my go-to preparations that utilize rhubarb, including this compote.

INGREDIENTS

1 cup (227 g) unsalted butter, softened

2 cups (400 g) sugar

5 (160 g) egg whites

1 teaspoon (4 g) vanilla paste

2⅔ cups (330 g) all-purpose flour

2½ teaspoons (11 g) baking powder

1 teaspoon (6 g) kosher salt

½ cup (120 ml) whole milk

½ cup (125 g) The Perfect Puree Strawberry Puree

1 to 2 drops of pink food coloring

Italian Meringue Buttercream (see page 29)

Strawberry Rhubarb Compote (see page 257), for filling

Preheat the oven to 325°F on convection mode or 350°F for a conventional oven. Line three cupcake pans with paper liners.

Place the butter and sugar in the work bowl of a stand mixer fitted with the paddle attachment and cream until the mixture is light and fluffy, 3 to 5 minutes. Scrape down the work bowl, add the egg whites and vanilla, and beat to incorporate.

Place the flour, baking powder, and salt in a bowl and whisk to combine. Sift the mixture through a fine-mesh tamis onto a piece of parchment paper. Fold the parchment paper lengthwise and alternate between adding small increments of the dry mixture, milk, and strawberry puree to the work bowl, beating to incorporate each addition and scraping down the work bowl as needed. Add the food coloring and beat to incorporate.

Transfer the batter to a piping bag, pipe it into the paper liners, and place the cupcakes in the oven. Bake until their internal temperature is 200°F, 20 to 25 minutes, rotating the pans halfway through.

Remove the cupcakes from the oven and let them rest in the pans for 5 minutes. Using an offset spatula, remove the cupcakes from the pans and transfer them to a cupcake holder. Cover them tightly and let them cool completely.

When the cupcakes have cooled completely and are ready to be frosted, prepare the buttercream.

Working from the tops of the cupcakes, remove their centers and fill them with the compote. Frost the cupcakes with the buttercream and serve.

STRAWBERRY RHUBARB CUPCAKES, SEE PAGE 131

Almond & Rhubarb Cupcakes

YIELD: 36 CUPCAKES / **ACTIVE TIME:** 20 MINUTES / **TOTAL TIME:** 50 MINUTES

If you topped these with just a bit of sanding sugar, this recipe could work in the morning as muffins. But hey, this is a cupcake book, and you can never have too much pink buttercream in your life.

INGREDIENTS

1 cup peeled and finely diced rhubarb

2 tablespoons (26 g) sugar

Almond cupcake batter (see page 53)

Swiss Meringue Buttercream (see page 31)

Preheat the oven to 325°F on convection mode or 350°F for a conventional oven. Line three cupcake pans with paper liners.

Place the rhubarb and sugar in a bowl and toss to combine. Set the rhubarb aside.

Prepare the batter, adding the rhubarb toward the end of the mixing process. Transfer the batter to a piping bag and pipe it into the paper liners. Place the cupcakes in the oven and bake until their internal temperature is 200°F, 20 to 25 minutes, rotating the pans halfway through.

Remove the cupcakes from the oven and let them rest in the pans for 5 minutes. Using an offset spatula, remove the cupcakes from the pans and transfer them to a cupcake holder. Cover them tightly and let them cool completely.

When the cupcakes have cooled completely and are ready to be frosted, prepare the buttercream.

Frost the cupcakes with the buttercream and serve.

Blackberry Crumble Cupcakes

YIELD: 36 CUPCAKES / **ACTIVE TIME:** 20 MINUTES / **TOTAL TIME:** 50 MINUTES

I find blackberries to be seriously underutilized in desserts, as they are my favorite berry to cook with. Super versatile, super resilient, and super healthy! At least that's what I tell myself when I make these.

INGREDIENTS

FOR THE CUPCAKES

White Cupcake Batter
(see page 35)

1½ tablespoons (10.5 g) Spice
Girl Mix (see page 254)

72 to 108 blackberries, plus
more for topping

2 tablespoons (26 g) sugar

FOR THE BUTTERCREAM

Swiss Meringue
Buttercream (see page 31)

½ cup (125 g) The Perfect
Puree Blackberry Puree

Oat Crumble (see page 258),
for topping

Preheat the oven to 325°F on convection mode or 350°F for a conventional oven. Line three cupcake pans with paper liners.

To begin preparations for the cupcakes, prepare the batter, adding the Spice Girl Mix along with the other dry ingredients. Place the blackberries in a bowl, sprinkle the sugar over them, and toss to coat. Add the blackberries to the batter and fold until they are evenly distributed. Transfer the batter to a piping bag and pipe it into the paper liners.

Place the cupcakes in the oven and bake until their internal temperature is 200°F, 20 to 25 minutes, rotating the pans halfway through.

Remove the cupcakes from the oven and let them rest in the pans for 5 minutes. Using an offset spatula, remove the cupcakes from the pans and transfer them to a cupcake holder. Cover them tightly and let them cool completely.

When the cupcakes have cooled completely and are ready to be frosted, prepare the Swiss Meringue Buttercream. Add the blackberry puree and beat to incorporate.

Frost the cupcakes with the blackberry buttercream, sprinkle the Oat Crumble over the top, top with additional blackberries, and serve.

Lemon, Lavender & Blueberry Cupcakes

YIELD: 36 CUPCAKES / **ACTIVE TIME:** 20 MINUTES / **TOTAL TIME:** 50 MINUTES

Lemon with lavender, lavender with blueberry, blueberry with lemon, this one just makes sense. I once had a chef tell me lavender doesn't belong in desserts, but I simply disagree, as its sweet and herbal notes pair super well with the brightness of lemon.

INGREDIENTS

FOR THE CUPCAKES

1½ cups (220 g) frozen blueberries

All-purpose flour, as needed

Butter Cupcake Batter (see page 36)

Zest of 2 lemons

2½ tablespoons (14 g) dried lavender, chopped

FOR THE BUTTERCREAM

French Meringue Buttercream (see page 30)

½ cup (113 ml) reduced juices from Blueberry Compote (see page 254)

Blueberry Compote, for filling

Lemon curd (see page 73), for topping

Preheat the oven to 325°F on convection mode or 350°F for a conventional oven. Line three cupcake pans with paper liners.

To begin preparations for the cupcakes, place the frozen blueberries in a bowl, sprinkle flour over them, and toss to coat. Set the blueberries aside.

Prepare the batter, adding the lemon zest, lavender, and blueberries toward the end of the mixing process. Transfer it to a piping bag and pipe the batter into the paper liners.

Place the cupcakes in the oven and bake until their internal temperature is 200°F, 20 to 25 minutes, rotating the pans halfway through.

Remove the cupcakes from the oven and let them rest in the pans for 5 minutes. Using an offset spatula, remove the cupcakes from the pans and transfer them to a cupcake holder. Cover them tightly and let them cool completely.

When the cupcakes have cooled completely and are ready to be frosted, prepare the French Meringue Buttercream. Add the reduced blueberry liquid and beat to incorporate.

Working from the bottoms of the cupcakes, remove their centers and fill them with the Blueberry Compote. Frost them with the blueberry buttercream, top them with the lemon curd, and serve.

Honey Cupcakes

YIELD: 24 CUPCAKES / **ACTIVE TIME:** 20 MINUTES / **TOTAL TIME:** 50 MINUTES

Honey is one of my favorite flavors to work with when making cakes, as it enhances taste, texture, and appearance, keeps them moist, is a natural sweetener, and balances the fats in buttercream.

INGREDIENTS

1½ cups (330 g) sugar

1 cup (226 g) unsalted butter, softened

4 (232 g) eggs

3 cups (375 g) all-purpose flour

2 teaspoons (9 g) baking powder

1 teaspoon (6 g) kosher salt

1 cup (224 ml) buttermilk

½ cup (170 g) honey

2 teaspoons (9 g) vanilla paste

Honey buttercream (see page 49)

Fresh honeycomb, for topping

Preheat the oven to 325°F on convection mode or 350°F in a conventional oven. Line two cupcake pans with paper liners.

Place the sugar and butter in the work bowl of a stand mixer fitted with the paddle attachment and cream until the mixture is light and fluffy, 3 to 5 minutes. Scrape down the work bowl, add the eggs one at a time, and beat to incorporate.

Place the flour, baking powder, and salt in a bowl and whisk to combine. Sift the mixture through a fine-mesh tamis onto a piece of parchment paper. Place the buttermilk, honey, and vanilla in a separate bowl and whisk to combine. Fold the parchment paper lengthwise and alternate between adding small increments of the dry mixture and buttermilk mixture to the work bowl, beating to incorporate each addition and scraping down the work bowl as needed.

Transfer the batter to a piping bag, pipe it into the paper liners, and place the cupcakes in the oven. Bake until their internal temperature is 200°F, 20 to 25 minutes, rotating the pans halfway through.

Remove the cupcakes from the oven and let them rest in the pans for 5 minutes. Using an offset spatula, remove the cupcakes from the pans and transfer them to a cupcake holder. Cover them tightly and let them cool completely.

When the cupcakes have cooled completely and are ready to be frosted, prepare the buttercream.

Frost the cupcakes with the honey buttercream, top them with fresh honeycomb, and serve.

Pistachio Cupcakes

YIELD: 18 CUPCAKES / **ACTIVE TIME:** 20 MINUTES / **TOTAL TIME:** 50 MINUTES

There are two kinds of pistachio paste out there: flavored and colored, or natural. When creating treats with higher fat content, like ice creams, mousses, and buttercreams, I prefer to use the flavored and colored variety, as it supplies the color and flavor that are associated with pistachio.

INGREDIENTS

FOR THE CUPCAKES

¾ cup (175 g) sugar

⅓ cup (85 g) unsalted butter, softened

1 cup (130 g) raw pistachios

1 cup (140 g) cake flour

1 teaspoon (4.5 g) baking powder

¼ teaspoon (1 g) baking soda

½ teaspoon (3 g) kosher salt

3 (126 g) egg whites

¼ cup (60 g) sour cream

1 teaspoon (4 g) vanilla paste

½ cup (120 ml) milk

FOR THE BUTTERCREAM

Big Fish Buttercream (see page 28)

½ cup (113 g) Fabbri Pistachio Delipaste

Candied Pistachios (see page 258), for topping

Preheat the oven to 325°F on convection mode or 350°F in a conventional oven. Line two cupcake pans with paper liners.

To begin preparations for the cupcakes, place the sugar and butter in the work bowl of a stand mixer fitted with the paddle attachment and cream until the mixture is light and fluffy, 3 to 5 minutes. While you are creaming the butter and sugar, place the pistachios, flour, baking powder, baking soda, and salt in a food processor and blitz until the mixture is a fine meal.

Add the egg whites, sour cream, and vanilla to the work bowl and beat to incorporate. Alternate between adding small increments of the pistachio mixture and milk to the work bowl, beating to incorporate each addition and scraping down the work bowl as needed.

Transfer the batter to a piping bag, pipe it into the paper liners, and place the cupcakes in the oven. Bake until their internal temperature is 200°F, 20 to 25 minutes, rotating the pans halfway through.

Remove the cupcakes from the oven and let them rest in the pans for 5 minutes. Using an offset spatula, remove the cupcakes from the pans and transfer them to a cupcake holder. Cover them tightly and let them cool completely.

When the cupcakes have cooled completely and are ready to be frosted, prepare the Big Fish Buttercream. Add the pistachio paste and beat until it has emulsified.

Frost the cupcakes with the buttercream, top them with the Candied Pistachios, and serve.

Lemon Poppy Seed Cupcakes

YIELD: 18 CUPCAKES / **ACTIVE TIME:** 30 MINUTES / **TOTAL TIME:** 1 HOUR

A recipe I've been making since I first started in pastry, and one my then mentor, now business and life partner, Derek, developed and then shared with me. This may be hard to believe, but Derek is a way better baker than I am. I was always drawn more to the pastry side of things, where Derek had a better understanding and patience for the art of baking. His recipe gets an intense lemon flavor from a reduction, and the poppy seeds don't stick in your teeth because they are soaked in milk overnight and softened.

INGREDIENTS

Lemon poppy seed cupcake batter (see page 66)

Big Fish Buttercream (see page 28)

Lemon curd (see page 73), for filling

Preheat the oven to 325°F on convection mode or 350°F for a conventional oven. Line two cupcake pans with paper liners.

Prepare the batter, transfer it to a piping bag, and pipe the batter into the paper liners. Place the cupcakes in the oven and bake until their internal temperature is 200°F, 20 to 25 minutes, rotating the pans halfway through.

Remove the cupcakes from the oven and let them rest in the pans for 5 minutes. Using an offset spatula, remove the cupcakes from the pans and transfer them to a cupcake holder. Cover them tightly and let them cool completely.

When the cupcakes have cooled completely and are ready to be frosted, prepare the buttercream.

Working from the tops of the cupcakes, remove their centers and fill them with the lemon curd. Frost the cupcakes with the buttercream and serve.

Strawberry & Basil Cupcakes

YIELD: 24 CUPCAKES / **ACTIVE TIME:** 25 MINUTES / **TOTAL TIME:** 50 MINUTES

These cupcakes are filled with a fruity, earthy, and spring-forward flavor. In Maine, strawberry season lasts only a few short weeks, and since our weather is so unpredictable, freeze-dried strawberries are a much safer option to achieve the right color and flavor.

INGREDIENTS

FOR THE CUPCAKES

Olive oil cupcake batter (see page 130)

1 tablespoon (1.2 g) finely chopped fresh basil

FOR THE BUTTERCREAM

1 cup (226 g) unsalted butter, softened

1 cup (25 g) freeze-dried strawberries

4 cups (480 g) confectioners' sugar

¼ cup (60 ml) heavy cream

1 teaspoon (4 g) vanilla paste

Pinch of kosher salt

Preheat the oven to 325°F on convection mode or 350°F for a conventional oven. Line two cupcake pans with paper liners.

To begin preparations for the cupcakes, prepare the batter, adding the basil toward the end of the mixing process.

Transfer the batter to a piping bag and pipe the batter into the paper liners. Place the cupcakes in the oven and bake until their internal temperature is 200°F, 20 to 25 minutes, rotating the pans halfway through.

Remove the cupcakes from the oven and let them rest in the pans for 5 minutes. Using an offset spatula, remove the cupcakes from the pans and transfer them to a cupcake holder. Cover them tightly and let them cool completely.

When the cupcakes are completely cool and ready to be frosted, prepare the buttercream. Place the butter in the work bowl of a stand mixer fitted with the paddle attachment and beat until it is light and fluffy, about 4 minutes. While the butter is being beaten, use a spice grinder or a mortar and pestle to grind the strawberries into a fine powder. Add the strawberry powder and confectioners' sugar to the work bowl and beat to incorporate. Add the cream, vanilla, and salt and beat to incorporate.

Frost the cupcakes with the strawberry buttercream and serve.

SUMMER

$\mathcal{N}$o matter how outsized the sweet tooth, in summer one does not want to feel weighed down, laden with rich, heavy foods. Which makes cupcakes the perfect choice for dessert during this season. Light, airy, and miniature, they ensure that you'll have no trouble soaking up the sun and at the same time soothing the sweet cravings that do not give one thought to the time of year or the temperature outside.

Watermelon Cupcakes

YIELD: 36 CUPCAKES / **ACTIVE TIME:** 20 MINUTES / **TOTAL TIME:** 50 MINUTES

If you want to go the whole way and capture the look of the watermelon, use metallic black sprinkles for the seeds—the result would be perfect for a summer neighborhood block party.

INGREDIENTS

FOR THE CUPCAKES

White Cupcake Batter
(see page 35)

3 drops of pink food coloring

2 tablespoons (26 ml)
LorAnn Watermelon Flavor

FOR THE BUTTERCREAM

Swiss Meringue
Buttercream (see page 31)

1 teaspoon (4 g) LorAnn
Watermelon Flavor

Preheat the oven to 325°F on convection mode or 350°F for a conventional oven. Line three cupcake pans with paper liners.

To begin preparations for the cupcakes, prepare the batter, adding the food coloring and watermelon flavor toward the end of the mixing process. Transfer it to a piping bag and pipe the batter into the paper liners.

Place the cupcakes in the oven and bake until their internal temperature is 200°F, 20 to 25 minutes, rotating the pans halfway through.

Remove the cupcakes from the oven and let them rest in the pans for 5 minutes. Using an offset spatula, remove the cupcakes from the pans and transfer them to a cupcake holder. Cover them tightly and let them cool completely.

When the cupcakes are completely cool and ready to be frosted, prepare the Swiss Meringue Buttercream. Add the watermelon flavor and beat to incorporate.

Frost the cupcakes with the watermelon buttercream and serve.

Margarita Cupcakes

YIELD: 36 CUPCAKES / **ACTIVE TIME:** 20 MINUTES / **TOTAL TIME:** 50 MINUTES

PSA: I do not recommend filling a pitcher with these. But I do recommend making a double batch.

INGREDIENTS

FOR THE CUPCAKES

White Cupcake Batter
(see page 35)

Zest of 2 limes

FOR THE FILLING

¾ sheet (1.9 g) of silver gelatin

2 (108 g) eggs

¼ cup (54 g) tequila

½ cup (108 ml) fresh lime juice

½ cup (108 g) sugar

9¾ tablespoons (140 g) unsalted butter, softened

French Meringue Buttercream (see page 30)

Preheat the oven to 325°F on convection mode or 350°F for a conventional oven. Line three cupcake pans with paper liners.

To begin preparations for the cupcakes, prepare the batter, adding the lime zest toward the end of the mixing process. Transfer it to a piping bag and pipe the batter into the paper liners.

Place the cupcakes in the oven and bake until their internal temperature is 200°F, 20 to 25 minutes, rotating the pans halfway through.

Remove the cupcakes from the oven and let them rest in the pans for 5 minutes. Using an offset spatula, remove the cupcakes from the pans and transfer them to a cupcake holder. Cover them tightly and let them cool completely.

To begin preparations for the filling, submerge the gelatin sheet in cold water and let it bloom for 6 minutes. Place the eggs, tequila, lime juice, and sugar in a small saucepan and warm the mixture over medium heat, whisking continually, until it is 170°F.

Transfer the mixture to a blender, add the bloomed gelatin and butter, and puree until the mixture is smooth and creamy. Transfer the curd to a bowl and place plastic wrap directly on the surface to prevent a skin from forming. Let the curd cool.

When the cupcakes are completely cool and ready to be filled and frosted, prepare the buttercream.

Working from the tops of the cupcakes, remove their centers and fill them with the tequila lime curd. Frost the cupcakes with the buttercream and serve.

Sherbet Cupcakes

YIELD: 36 CUPCAKES / **ACTIVE TIME:** 20 MINUTES / **TOTAL TIME:** 50 MINUTES

Even saying the word sherbet evokes memories of summertime in childhood. With the key notes being sweet berries and citrus, the addition of the sherbet extract helps to enhance this nostalgic treat.

INGREDIENTS

FOR THE CUPCAKES

White Cupcake Batter
(see page 35)

Zest of 3 limes

Zest of 2 lemons

Zest of 1 orange

2 tablespoons (26 ml)
Hobbyland Rainbow
Sherbet Flavoring

FOR THE BUTTERCREAM

Swiss Meringue
Buttercream (see page 31)

2 tablespoons (26 ml)
Hobbyland Rainbow
Sherbet Flavoring

Preheat the oven to 325°F on convection mode or 350°F for a conventional oven. Line three cupcake pans with paper liners.

To begin preparations for the cupcakes, prepare the batter, adding the zests and sherbet flavoring toward the end of the mixing process. Transfer it to a piping bag and pipe the batter into the paper liners.

Place the cupcakes in the oven and bake until their internal temperature is 200°F, 20 to 25 minutes, rotating the pans halfway through.

Remove the cupcakes from the oven and let them rest in the pans for 5 minutes. Using an offset spatula, remove the cupcakes from the pans and transfer them to a cupcake holder. Cover them tightly and let them cool completely.

When the cupcakes are completely cool and ready to be frosted, prepare the Swiss Meringue Buttercream. Add the sherbet flavoring and beat to incorporate.

Frost the cupcakes with the sherbet buttercream and serve.

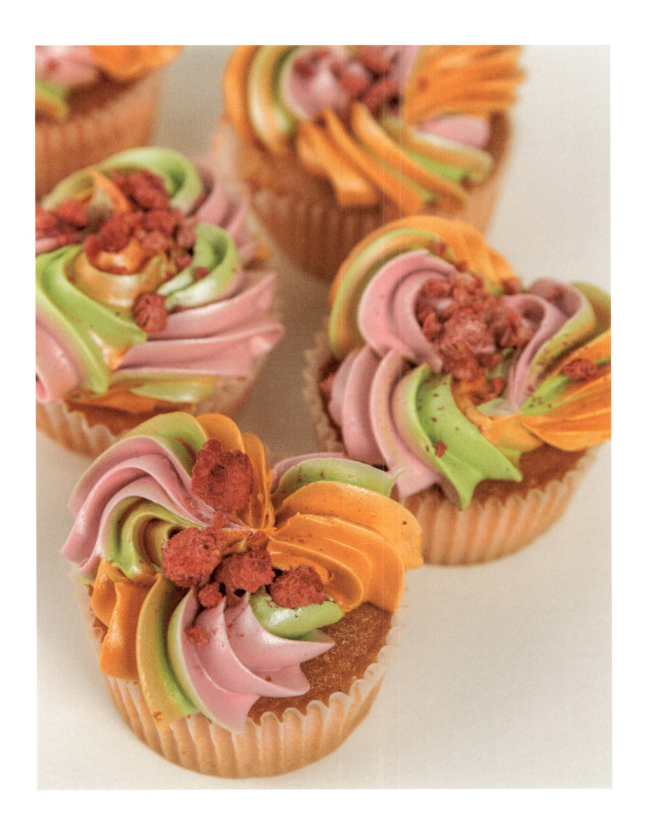

Strawberry Lemonade Cupcakes

YIELD: 24 CUPCAKES / **ACTIVE TIME:** 20 MINUTES / **TOTAL TIME:** 50 MINUTES

These cupcakes are a great spot to start testing your decorating skills. I garnished these with pink pearls to resemble the bubbles in this summery drink, but also played with this sweet color scheme. You could experiment with different piping tips, and garnish with either candied lemon, fresh strawberries, or sprinkles to hide any imperfections.

INGREDIENTS

Strawberry cupcake batter (see page 131)

3 tablespoons (18 g) lemon zest

Strawberry buttercream (see page 147)

Preheat the oven to 325°F on convection mode or 350°F for a conventional oven. Line two cupcake pans with paper liners.

Prepare the batter, adding the lemon zest toward the end of the mixing process. Transfer it to a piping bag and pipe the batter into the paper liners. Place the cupcakes in the oven and bake until their internal temperature is 200°F, 20 to 25 minutes, rotating the pans halfway through.

Remove the cupcakes from the oven and let them rest in the pans for 5 minutes. Using an offset spatula, remove the cupcakes from the pans and transfer them to a cupcake holder. Cover them tightly and let them cool completely.

When the cupcakes are completely cool and ready to be frosted, prepare the buttercream.

Frost the cupcakes with the strawberry buttercream and serve.

Rum Baba Cupcakes

YIELD: 36 CUPCAKES / **ACTIVE TIME:** 25 MINUTES / **TOTAL TIME:** 50 MINUTES

The classic Baba au Rhum originated in France, but it's a well-traveled dessert that has been modified by many cultures, so I saw an avenue to make my own spin on it. I like to use a Jamaican spiced rum here, and serve these with tropical fruit.

Preheat the oven to 325°F on convection mode or 350°F for a conventional oven. Line three cupcake pans with paper liners.

To prepare the syrup, place the butter, water, sugar, and rum in a medium saucepan and bring to a boil over medium heat, stirring to dissolve the sugar. Cook until the mixture has reduced by one-third, remove the pan from heat, and stir in the vanilla and salt. Let the syrup cool to room temperature and then store it in the refrigerator.

To begin preparations for the cupcakes, place the flour, sugar, instant pudding mix, butter, canola oil, salt, vanilla, and baking powder in the work bowl of a stand mixer fitted with the paddle attachment and beat until the mixture has a sandy consistency, about 2 minutes. With the mixer running, slowly stream in the milk and beat to incorporate.

Scrape down the work bowl, add the eggs one at a time, and beat to incorporate. Scrape down the work bowl. With the mixer running, slowly stream in the rum and beat to incorporate.

Transfer the batter to a piping bag and pipe the batter into the paper liners. Place the cupcakes in the oven and bake until their internal temperature is 200°F, 20 to 25 minutes, rotating the pans halfway through.

Remove the cupcakes from the oven and let them rest in the pans for 5 minutes. Using an offset spatula, remove the cupcakes from the pans and transfer them to a cupcake holder. Cover them tightly and let them cool completely.

When the cupcakes are completely cool and ready to be frosted, prepare the buttercream.

Gently dip the tops of the cupcakes into the syrup and let the cupcakes absorb the syrup for a few seconds. Frost them with the buttercream and serve.

INGREDIENTS

FOR THE SYRUP

½ cup (113 g) unsalted butter

¼ cup (57 ml) water

1 cup (198 g) sugar

½ cup (113 ml) rum

1 (4 g) teaspoon vanilla paste

Pinch of kosher salt

FOR THE CUPCAKES

3¾ cups (480 g) all-purpose flour

3 cups (596 g) sugar

6.8 oz. (192.7 g) instant vanilla pudding mix

1 cup (226 g) unsalted butter, softened

1 cup (198 ml) canola oil

1 teaspoon (6 g) kosher salt

1 tablespoon (12 g) vanilla paste

4 teaspoons (16 g) baking powder

1 cup (226 ml) whole milk

8 (440 g) eggs

1 cup (226 ml) rum

French Meringue Buttercream (see page 30)

Aperol Spritz Cupcakes

YIELD: 36 CUPCAKES / **ACTIVE TIME:** 20 MINUTES / **TOTAL TIME:** 50 MINUTES

The ever-trendy cocktail turned into a dessert. Slip into a matching dress and you'll be the hostess with the moistest.

INGREDIENTS

Butter Cupcake Batter (see page 36)

Zest of 3 oranges

French Meringue Buttercream (see page 30)

Preheat the oven to 325°F on convection mode or 350°F for a conventional oven. Line three cupcake pans with paper liners.

Prepare the batter, adding the zest toward the end of the mixing process. Transfer it to a piping bag and pipe the batter into the paper liners. Place the cupcakes in the oven and bake until their internal temperature is 200°F, 20 to 25 minutes, rotating the pans halfway through.

Remove the cupcakes from the oven and let them rest in the pans for 5 minutes. Using an offset spatula, remove the cupcakes from the pans and transfer them to a cupcake holder. Cover them tightly and let them cool completely.

When the cupcakes are completely cool and ready to be frosted, prepare the buttercream.

Frost the cupcakes with the buttercream and serve.

Bourbon & Peach Cupcakes

YIELD: 36 CUPCAKES / **ACTIVE TIME:** 20 MINUTES / **TOTAL TIME:** 50 MINUTES

Sweet, buttery, and smooth, this cupcake recipe hits all my favorite notes and textures. Try to find peaches that are hard enough to cut but ripe enough where you can taste their natural sweetness. I decided to use a LorAnn oil here because hard liquor in foods should be used in moderation, and I wanted to enhance the flavors but keep them from being overwhelming.

INGREDIENTS

FOR THE CUPCAKES

Butter Cupcake Batter (see page 36)

1 teaspoon (4 ml) LorAnn Bourbon Flavor

FOR THE BUTTERCREAM

Big Fish Buttercream (see page 28)

1 tablespoon (13 g) LorAnn Peach Flavor

Bourbon & Peach Compote (see page 258), for filling

Preheat the oven to 325°F on convection mode or 350°F for a conventional oven. Line three cupcake pans with paper liners.

To begin preparations for the cupcakes, prepare the batter, adding the bourbon flavor toward the end of the mixing process. Transfer it to a piping bag and pipe the batter into the paper liners.

Place the cupcakes in the oven and bake until their internal temperature is 200°F, 20 to 25 minutes, rotating the pans halfway through.

Remove the cupcakes from the oven and let them rest in the pans for 5 minutes. Using an offset spatula, remove the cupcakes from the pans and transfer them to a cupcake holder. Cover them tightly and let them cool completely.

When the cupcakes are completely cool and ready to be frosted, prepare the Big Fish Buttercream. Add the peach flavor and beat to incorporate.

Working from the bottoms of the cupcakes, remove their centers and fill them with the compote. Frost the cupcakes with the peach buttercream and serve.

Hibiscus Cupcakes

YIELD: 36 CUPCAKES / **ACTIVE TIME:** 20 MINUTES / **TOTAL TIME:** 50 MINUTES

The earthy and berry notes of hibiscus make it so fun to play around with in the kitchen. Add in the beautiful magenta hues it supplies, and it's sure to produce a winner.

INGREDIENTS

FOR THE CUPCAKES

Vanilla Cupcake Batter
(see page 34)

3 tablespoons (24 g) hibiscus powder

FOR THE FILLING

White Chocolate Ganache
(see page 257)

2 tablespoons (16 g) hibiscus powder

Swiss Meringue
Buttercream (see page 31)

Preheat the oven to 325°F on convection mode or 350°F for a conventional oven. Line three cupcake pans with paper liners.

To begin preparations for the cupcakes, prepare the batter, adding the hibiscus powder with the dry ingredients. Transfer it to a piping bag and pipe the batter into the paper liners.

Place the cupcakes in the oven and bake until their internal temperature is 200°F, 20 to 25 minutes, rotating the pans halfway through.

Remove the cupcakes from the oven and let them rest in the pans for 5 minutes. Using an offset spatula, remove the cupcakes from the pans and transfer them to a cupcake holder. Cover them tightly and let them cool completely.

To prepare the filling, prepare the White Chocolate Ganache, stirring the hibiscus powder into the heavy-cream-and-glucose mixture when it is warm.

When the cupcakes are completely cool and ready to be frosted, prepare the buttercream.

Working from the tops of the cupcakes, remove their centers and fill them with the hibiscus ganache. Frost the cupcakes with the buttercream and serve.

Tres Leches Cupcakes

YIELD: 36 CUPCAKES / **ACTIVE TIME:** 20 MINUTES / **TOTAL TIME:** 50 MINUTES

The rare cupcake recipe that you can make ahead of time, as letting these cupcakes rest in the fridge will help them absorb the milks even more.

Preheat the oven to 325°F on convection mode or 350°F for a conventional oven. Line three cupcake pans with paper liners.

To begin preparations for the cupcakes, place the butter and sugar in the work bowl of a stand mixer fitted with the paddle attachment and cream until the mixture is pale and fluffy, 3 to 5 minutes. Scrape down the work bowl, add the eggs one at a time, and beat to incorporate.

Place the flour, baking powder, baking soda, salt, and Spice Girl Mix in a bowl and whisk to combine. Sift the mixture through a fine-mesh tamis onto a piece of parchment paper. Fold the parchment paper lengthwise and add small increments of the dry mixture to the work bowl, beating to incorporate each addition and scraping down the work bowl as needed. Add the vanilla and beat to incorporate.

Transfer the batter to a piping bag and pipe it into the paper liners.

Place the cupcakes in the oven and bake until their internal temperature is 200°F, 20 to 25 minutes, rotating the pans halfway through.

Remove the cupcakes from the oven and let them rest in the pans for 5 minutes. Using an offset spatula, remove the cupcakes from the pans and transfer them to a cupcake holder. Cover them tightly and let them cool completely.

When the cupcakes have cooled completely, prepare the tres leches. Place all of the ingredients in a bowl and whisk to combine.

Poke the tops of the cupcakes with a fork and spoon the tres leche over them. Top the cupcakes with the Chantilly and Sugared Berries and serve.

INGREDIENTS

FOR THE CUPCAKES

¾ cup (170 g) unsalted butter, softened

2 cups (400 g) sugar

4 (220 g) eggs

3¼ cups (445 g) cake flour

1¼ teaspoons (5.5 g) baking powder

1¼ teaspoons (5.5 g) baking soda

1¼ teaspoons (8 g) kosher salt

1 tablespoon (7 g) Spice Girl Mix (see page 254)

1½ teaspoons (6.5 g) vanilla paste

FOR THE TRES LECHES

1 (12 oz./340 ml) can of evaporated milk

½ (8.4 oz./240 ml) can of condensed milk

¾ cup (170 ml) heavy cream

Chantilly (see page 256), for topping

Sugared Berries (see page 258), for topping

Shirley Temple Cupcakes

YIELD: 36 CUPCAKES / **ACTIVE TIME:** 20 MINUTES / **TOTAL TIME:** 50 MINUTES

Glitter cherries are my new favorite garnish, and not just because of their ability to make these cupcakes feel even more iconic.

INGREDIENTS

Red velvet cupcake batter
(see page 57)

Italian Meringue
Buttercream (see page
29), with half of the water
replaced with grenadine

Edible glitter, as needed

Maraschino cherries,
for topping

Preheat the oven to 325°F on convection mode or 350°F for a conventional oven. Line three cupcake pans with paper liners.

Prepare the batter, transfer it to a piping bag, and pipe the batter into the paper liners.

Place the cupcakes in the oven and bake until their internal temperature is 200°F, 20 to 25 minutes, rotating the pans halfway through.

Remove the cupcakes from the oven and let them rest in the pans for 5 minutes. Using an offset spatula, remove the cupcakes from the pans and transfer them to a cupcake holder. Cover them tightly and let them cool completely.

When the cupcakes are completely cool and ready to be frosted, prepare the buttercream.

Frost the cupcakes with the grenadine buttercream. Place edible glitter in a shallow bowl and roll some cherries in it until they are completely coated. Top the cupcakes with the glitter cherries and serve.

Coconut & Mango Cupcakes

YIELD: 36 CUPCAKES / **ACTIVE TIME:** 20 MINUTES / **TOTAL TIME:** 50 MINUTES

Mango Ganache sunken inside these coconut cupcakes makes for a perfect, tropical bite. I topped these with Swiss Meringue Buttercream to balance the sweetness of the fruit, but if you wanted, adding a bit of mango puree to the emulsified buttercream and leaning entirely into that flavor is another solid idea.

INGREDIENTS

Coconut cupcake batter
(see page 61)

Swiss Meringue
Buttercream (see page 31)

Mango Ganache (see page
259), for filling

Preheat the oven to 325°F on convection mode or 350°F for a conventional oven. Line three cupcake pans with paper liners.

Prepare the batter, transfer it to a piping bag, and pipe the batter into the paper liners.

Place the cupcakes in the oven and bake until their internal temperature is 200°F, 20 to 25 minutes, rotating the pans halfway through.

Remove the cupcakes from the oven and let them rest in the pans for 5 minutes. Using an offset spatula, remove the cupcakes from the pans and transfer them to a cupcake holder. Cover them tightly and let them cool completely.

When the cupcakes are completely cool and ready to be frosted, prepare the buttercream.

Working from the tops of the cupcakes, remove their centers and fill them with the ganache. Frost the cupcakes with the buttercream and serve.

FALL

While autumn is not quite the baking season that winter is, it is not far behind. There is little better than taking a walk through the crisp evening air and coming home to warm yourself in the coziness of a kitchen where cupcakes are baking in the oven. Fall also makes some delectable flavors available that would not have appealed to one's palate a month or two before. From spicy chai–spiked cupcakes to those that center around the warmth of apple cider and pumpkin spice, this chapter has you covered when fall rolls around.

Carrot & Chai Cupcakes

YIELD: 24 CUPCAKES / **ACTIVE TIME:** 20 MINUTES / **TOTAL TIME:** 50 MINUTES

This isn't your traditional carrot cake, but rather the Big Fish version. Consider adding an extra pinch of salt to the chai buttercream, as I personally believe it takes things to another level.

INGREDIENTS

Carrot cupcake batter
(see page 58)

Big Fish Buttercream
(see page 28)

1½ tablespoons (12 g) Spice
Girl Mix (see page 254)

Apricot Jam (see page 259),
for filling

Preheat the oven to 325°F on convection mode or 350°F for a conventional oven. Line two cupcake pans with paper liners.

Prepare the batter, transfer it to a piping bag, and pipe it into the paper liners. Place the cupcakes in the oven and bake until their internal temperature is 200°F, 20 to 25 minutes, rotating the pans halfway through.

Remove the cupcakes from the oven and let them rest in the pans for 5 minutes. Using an offset spatula, remove the cupcakes from the pans and transfer them to a cupcake holder. Cover them tightly and let them cool completely.

When the cupcakes are completely cool and ready to be frosted, prepare the Big Fish Buttercream. Add the Spice Girl Mix and beat to incorporate.

Working from the tops of the cupcakes, remove their centers and fill them with the jam. Frost the cupcakes with the chai buttercream and serve.

Maple Pecan Cupcakes

YIELD: 36 CUPCAKES / **ACTIVE TIME:** 20 MINUTES / **TOTAL TIME:** 50 MINUTES

Maple and pecans complement each other so well because they are both so rich—a quality that comes out in the buttery flavor of pecans and the caramellike notes in maple syrup. The Dulce de Leche is just here to push your enjoyment over the top.

INGREDIENTS

Maple cupcake batter
(see page 82)

1½ cups (156 g) pecan pieces

Maple buttercream
(see page 82)

Dulce de Leche
(see page 255), for filling

Preheat the oven to 325°F on convection mode or 350°F for a conventional oven. Line three cupcake pans with paper liners.

Prepare the batter, adding the pecans toward the end of the mixing process. Transfer it to a piping bag and pipe the batter into the paper liners.

Place the cupcakes in the oven and bake until their internal temperature is 200°F, 20 to 25 minutes, rotating the pans halfway through.

Remove the cupcakes from the oven and let them rest in the pans for 5 minutes. Using an offset spatula, remove the cupcakes from the pans and transfer them to a cupcake holder. Cover them tightly and let them cool completely.

When the cupcakes are completely cool and ready to be frosted, prepare the buttercream.

Working from the tops of the cupcakes, remove their centers and fill them with the Dulce de Leche. Frost the cupcakes with the maple buttercream and serve.

Caramel Apple Cupcakes

YIELD: 18 CUPCAKES / **ACTIVE TIME:** 20 MINUTES / **TOTAL TIME:** 50 MINUTES

A crowd-pleaser that will fit in comfortably at any of your fall festivities. Best of all, you don't have to worry about breaking your teeth on a real caramel apple.

INGREDIENTS

½ cup (113 g) unsalted butter, softened

⅔ cup (135 g) brown sugar

⅓ cup (80 ml) milk

2 (116 g) eggs

2 teaspoons (9 g) vanilla paste

⅓ cup (75 g) sugar

1½ cups (190 g) all-purpose flour

¼ teaspoon (1 g) baking powder

1 teaspoon (6 g) baking soda

½ teaspoon (3 g) kosher salt

2 teaspoons (4.5 g) Spice Girl Mix (see page 254)

1½ apples, skin-on and finely diced

Caramel buttercream (see page 98)

Apple Chips (see page 259), for topping

Preheat the oven to 325°F on convection mode or 350°F for a conventional oven. Line two cupcake pans with paper liners.

Place the butter and brown sugar in a saucepan and melt them over medium heat. Transfer the mixture to a mixing bowl, add the milk, eggs, vanilla, and sugar, and whisk until the mixture is smooth.

Sift the flour into a separate bowl, add the baking powder, baking soda, salt, and Spice Girl Mix, and whisk to combine. Add the dry mixture to the wet mixture and whisk until the resulting mixture comes together as a smooth batter. Add the apples and fold until they are evenly distributed.

Transfer the batter to a piping bag and pipe it into the paper liners. Place the cupcakes in the oven and bake until their internal temperature is 200°F, 20 to 25 minutes, rotating the pans halfway through.

Remove the cupcakes from the oven and let them rest in the pans for 5 minutes. Using an offset spatula, remove the cupcakes from the pans and transfer them to a cupcake holder. Cover them tightly and let them cool completely.

When the cupcakes are completely cool and ready to be frosted, prepare the buttercream.

Frost the cupcakes with the caramel buttercream, top them with Apple Chips, and serve.

Caramel Corn Cupcakes

YIELD: 24 CUPCAKES / **ACTIVE TIME:** 20 MINUTES / **TOTAL TIME:** 50 MINUTES

Pure state fair flavor right here. The Caramel Corn can be a little tricky to make at home, so don't hesitate to purchase some at a good old-school candy shop. Also, I personally prefer making it on the stovetop, but as some of my worst burns have come from making caramel, I'd stick to the baking method I suggest if you have not made it before.

INGREDIENTS

3½ cups (581 g) fresh corn kernels

4 (232 g) eggs

1½ cups (327 ml) canola oil

2 cups (400 g) sugar

1 tablespoon (15 g) fresh lemon juice

2½ cups (345 g) cake flour

2 teaspoons (9 g) baking powder

1 teaspoon (6 g) kosher salt

Big Fish Buttercream (see page 28)

¾ cup (150 g) melted butterscotch chips, cooled to 90°F

Caramel Corn (see page 260), for topping

Preheat the oven to 325°F on convection mode or 350°F for a conventional oven. Line two cupcake pans with paper liners.

Place the corn in a food processor and blitz until smooth, about 2 minutes. In the work bowl of a stand mixer fitted with the whisk attachment, whip the eggs, canola oil, sugar, and lemon juice until the mixture is pale and fluffy, about 3 minutes.

Place the flour, baking powder, and salt in a bowl and whisk to combine. Sift the mixture through a fine-mesh tamis onto a piece of parchment paper. Fold the parchment paper lengthwise and alternate between adding small increments of the dry mixture and corn puree to the work bowl, beating to incorporate each addition and scraping down the work bowl as needed.

Transfer the batter to a piping bag, pipe it into the paper liners, and place the cupcakes in the oven. Bake until their internal temperature is 200°F, 20 to 25 minutes, rotating the pans halfway through.

Remove the cupcakes from the oven and let them rest in the pans for 5 minutes. Using an offset spatula, remove the cupcakes from the pans and transfer them to a cupcake holder. Cover them tightly and let them cool completely.

When the cupcakes are completely cool and ready to be frosted, prepare the Big Fish Buttercream. Add the melted butterscotch chips and beat until they have emulsified.

Frost the cupcakes with the butterscotch buttercream, top them with Caramel Corn, and serve.

Chai Latte Cupcakes

YIELD: 24 CUPCAKES / **ACTIVE TIME:** 20 MINUTES / **TOTAL TIME:** 50 MINUTES

Fats, coffee, and spice—as you've probably figured out by this point, these are three of my favorite things.

INGREDIENTS

FOR THE CUPCAKES

Butter Cupcake Batter
(see page 36)

2 tablespoons (26 ml) Trablit
Coffee Extract

2 tablespoons (14 g) Spice
Girl Mix (see page 254)

FOR THE TOPPING

8.8 oz. (250 ml) whole milk

1 cup (82 g) whole coffee
beans

1¼ oz. (25 g) sugar

½ teaspoon (2 g) vanilla
paste

1 sheet (2.2 g) of silver
gelatin

4 teaspoons (4 g) Foam
Magic

Preheat the oven to 325°F on convection mode or 350°F for a conventional oven. Line two cupcake pans with paper liners.

To begin preparations for the cupcakes, prepare the batter, adding the coffee extract with the milk and the Spice Girl Mix with the dry ingredients. Transfer it to a piping bag and pipe the batter into the paper liners.

Place the cupcakes in the oven and bake until their internal temperature is 200°F, 20 to 25 minutes, rotating the pans halfway through.

Remove the cupcakes from the oven and let them rest in the pans for 5 minutes. Using an offset spatula, remove the cupcakes from the pans and transfer them to a cupcake holder. Cover them tightly and let them cool completely.

To begin preparations for the topping, submerge the gelatin sheet in cold water and let it bloom for 6 minutes. Place the milk in a small saucepan and bring to a simmer. Add the coffee beans and steep for 10 minutes.

Strain the milk, stir in the sugar and vanilla, and chill the mixture in the refrigerator for 30 minutes.

Remove the milk mixture from the refrigerator and stir in the Foam Magic. Use an immersion blender to create foam.

Spoon the foam over the cupcakes and serve immediately.

Orange & Cranberry Cupcakes

YIELD: 36 CUPCAKES / **ACTIVE TIME:** 25 MINUTES / **TOTAL TIME:** 50 MINUTES

Cranberries, known for their tartness, tanginess, and bitter skin, are rarely found in desserts, but with the right amount of sugar and acid to counterbalance those qualities, they make for another festive fall flavor.

INGREDIENTS

FOR THE CUPCAKES

Vanilla Cupcake Batter
(see page 34)

Zest of 2 oranges

1 cup (120 g) fresh
cranberries

FOR THE BUTTERCREAM

1 cup (120 g) fresh
cranberries

½ cup (108 ml) orange juice

¼ cup (50 g) sugar

Big Fish Buttercream
(see page 28)

Candied Cranberries
(see page 260), for topping

Preheat the oven to 325°F on convection mode or 350°F for a conventional oven. Line three cupcake pans with paper liners.

To begin preparations for the cupcakes, prepare the batter, adding the orange zest and cranberries toward the end of the mixing process. Transfer it to a piping bag and pipe the batter into the paper liners.

Place the cupcakes in the oven and bake until their internal temperature is 200°F, 20 to 25 minutes, rotating the pans halfway through.

Remove the cupcakes from the oven and let them rest in the pans for 5 minutes. Using an offset spatula, remove the cupcakes from the pans and transfer them to a cupcake holder. Cover them tightly and let them cool completely.

When the cupcakes are completely cool and ready to be frosted, begin preparations for the buttercream. Place the cranberries, orange juice, and sugar in a medium saucepan and bring to a boil. Cook, stirring occasionally, until the sugar has dissolved, the cranberries have popped, and the juices start to thicken.

Using an immersion blender, puree the mixture until smooth. Strain the syrup into a bowl and let it cool to 90°F.

Prepare the Big Fish Buttercream. Add the syrup to the buttercream and beat until it has emulsified.

Frost the cupcakes with the orange and cranberry buttercream, top them with Candied Cranberries, and serve.

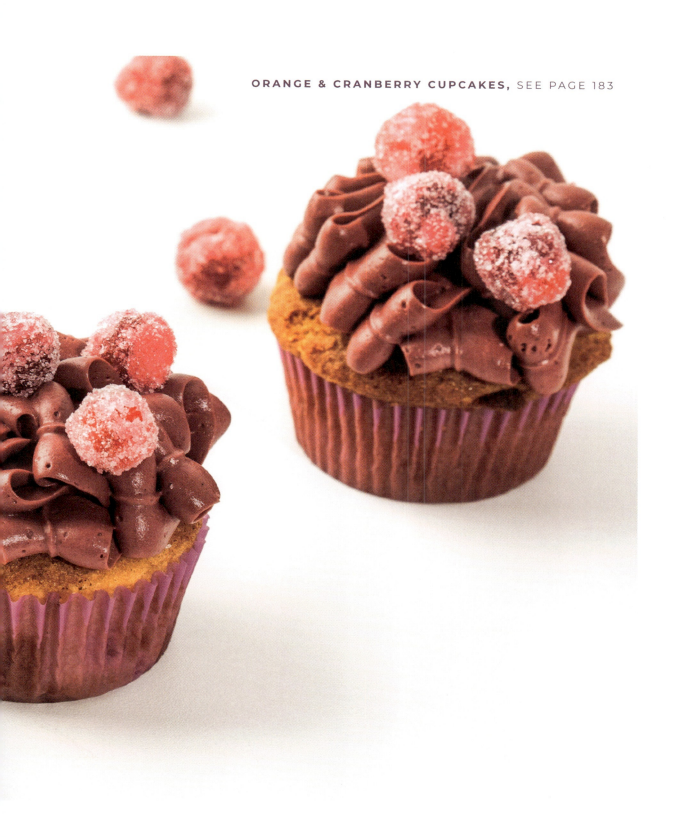

ORANGE & CRANBERRY CUPCAKES, SEE PAGE 183

Cider Cupcakes

YIELD: 12 CUPCAKES / **ACTIVE TIME:** 25 MINUTES / **TOTAL TIME:** 50 MINUTES

This cider reduction and the Apple Butter are great ways to utilize bruised apples or cider that is about to go off, as both supply a wonderful concentrated apple flavor and lovely texture.

To begin preparations for the cupcakes, place the apple cider in a medium saucepan and bring to a simmer over medium heat. Cook until it has reduced to ¾ cup. Remove the pan from heat and let the reduced cider cool completely.

Preheat the oven to 325°F on convection mode or 350°F for a conventional oven. Line a cupcake pan with paper liners.

Place the canola oil, brown sugar, reduced cider, and vanilla in a mixing bowl and whisk to combine.

Sift the flour into a separate bowl, add the baking powder, baking soda, and Spice Girl Mix, and whisk to combine. Add the dry mixture to the wet mixture and whisk until the resulting mixture comes together as a smooth batter. Add the apple and fold until it is evenly distributed.

Transfer the batter to a piping bag and pipe it into the paper liners. Place the cupcakes in the oven and bake until their internal temperature is 200°F, 20 to 25 minutes, rotating the pan halfway through.

Remove the cupcakes from the oven and let them rest in the pan for 5 minutes.

While the cupcakes are resting, place the sugar and cinnamon in a shallow bowl and whisk to combine. Using an offset spatula, remove the cupcakes from the pan and dip the tops into the cinnamon sugar until they are coated. Transfer the cupcakes to a cupcake holder, cover them tightly, and let them cool completely.

When the cupcakes are completely cool and ready to be frosted, prepare the Big Fish Buttercream. Add the cinnamon oil and cinnamon and beat until the oil has emulsified.

Working from the tops of the cupcakes, remove their centers and fill them with the Apple Butter. Frost the cupcakes with the cinnamon buttercream and serve.

INGREDIENTS

FOR THE CUPCAKES

2 cups (454 ml) apple cider

½ cup (125 ml) canola oil

¾ cup (150 g) brown sugar

2 teaspoons (9 g) vanilla paste

1½ cups (180 g) all-purpose flour

½ teaspoon (2 g) baking powder

¼ teaspoon (1 g) baking soda

2 teaspoons (5 g) Spice Girl Mix (see page 254)

1 (85 g) apple, peeled and diced

½ cup (100 g) sugar

½ teaspoon (1.5 g) cinnamon

FOR THE BUTTERCREAM

Big Fish Buttercream (see page 28)

¼ teaspoon (1 ml) LorAnn Cinnamon Oil

½ teaspoon (1.5 g) cinnamon

Apple Butter (see page 260), for filling

INGREDIENTS

FOR THE CUPCAKES

1 cup (227 g) unsalted butter, softened

2½ cups (550 g) brown sugar

4 (220 g) eggs

4 cups (548 g) cake flour

1⅓ tablespoons (18 g) baking powder

1 teaspoon (4 g) baking soda

1 teaspoon (6 g) kosher salt

2½ tablespoons (19 g) Spice Girl Mix (see page 254)

1 cup (238 ml) buttermilk

1½ cups (238 g) pumpkin puree

FOR THE BUTTERCREAM

1½ cups (340 g) cream cheese, softened

½ cup (113 g) unsalted butter, softened

4 cups (480 g) confectioners' sugar

1½ teaspoons (4 g) cinnamon

⅓ cup (82 g) pumpkin puree

½ teaspoon (2 g) vanilla paste

Pumpkin Spice Cupcakes

YIELD: 30 CUPCAKES / **ACTIVE TIME:** 20 MINUTES / **TOTAL TIME:** 45 MINUTES

At the last minute I decided to add pumpkin to the buttercream as well, going all in for all you pumpkin people out there.

Preheat the oven to 325°F on convection mode or 350°F for a conventional oven. Line three cupcake pans with paper liners.

To begin preparations for the cupcakes, place the butter and brown sugar in the work bowl of a stand mixer fitted with the paddle attachment and cream until the mixture is pale and fluffy, 3 to 5 minutes. Scrape down the work bowl, add the eggs one at a time, and beat to incorporate.

Place the flour, baking powder, baking soda, salt, and Spice Girl Mix in a bowl and whisk to combine. Sift the mixture through a fine-mesh tamis onto a piece of parchment paper. Fold the parchment paper lengthwise and alternate between adding small increments of the dry mixture and buttermilk to the work bowl, beating to incorporate each addition and scraping down the work bowl as needed. Add the pumpkin and beat until it is just incorporated.

Transfer the batter to a piping bag and pipe it into the paper liners.

Place the cupcakes in the oven and bake until their internal temperature is 200°F, 20 to 25 minutes, rotating the pans halfway through.

Remove the cupcakes from the oven and let them rest in the pans for 5 minutes. Using an offset spatula, remove the cupcakes from the pans and transfer them to a cupcake holder. Cover them tightly and let them cool completely.

When the cupcakes have cooled completely and are ready to be frosted, prepare the buttercream. Place the cream cheese and butter in the work bowl of a stand mixer fitted with the paddle attachment and cream until the mixture is fluffy and not clumpy. Scrape down the work bowl, set the mixer to low, and gradually add the confectioners' sugar and cinnamon. Add the pumpkin and vanilla and beat to incorporate.

Frost the cupcakes with the pumpkin and cream cheese buttercream and serve.

WINTER

*B*akers are fortunate in that the winter is a little less harsh for them, giving them plenty of reason to stay inside and spend their time in the kitchen, turning out delicious treats. It is also nice because the miserable cold and dwindling light means that people will be in severe need of comfort, and so open to rich, decadent flavors and bold, spicy offerings that would seem insane to consider at other times of the year.

White Mocha Cupcakes

YIELD: 36 CUPCAKES / **ACTIVE TIME:** 20 MINUTES
TOTAL TIME: 1 HOUR AND 50 MINUTES

Once I discovered the art of infusing, I quickly became obsessed with working coffee-spiked liquids in wherever I could. The addition of white chocolate creates a white mocha that opens up endless possibilities, all of them delicious. If you'd like to give these a bit of crunch, top with some chocolate-covered espresso beans.

INGREDIENTS

½ cup (118 ml) whole milk

½ cup (41 g) whole coffee beans

White Cupcake Batter (see page 35)

White chocolate buttercream (see page 42)

White Chocolate Mocha Ganache (see page 261), for filling

Preheat the oven to 325°F on convection mode or 350°F for a conventional oven. Line three cupcake pans with paper liners.

Place the milk in a small saucepan and bring to a simmer. Add the coffee beans, cover the pan, and steep for 30 minutes.

Strain the milk and chill it in the refrigerator for 10 minutes.

Prepare the batter, adding the coffee milk toward the end of the mixing process. Transfer it to a piping bag and pipe the batter into the paper liners.

Place the cupcakes in the oven and bake until their internal temperature is 200°F, 20 to 25 minutes, rotating the pans halfway through.

Remove the cupcakes from the oven and let them rest in the pans for 5 minutes. Using an offset spatula, remove the cupcakes from the pans and transfer them to a cupcake holder. Cover them tightly and let them cool completely.

When the cupcakes are completely cool and ready to be frosted, prepare the buttercream.

Working from the tops of the cupcakes, remove their centers and fill them with the ganache. Frost the cupcakes with the white chocolate buttercream and serve.

Chocolate Stout Cupcakes

YIELD: 36 CUPCAKES / **ACTIVE TIME:** 20 MINUTES / **TOTAL TIME:** 50 MINUTES

The deep, roasted malt flavor of stout beer enhances the richness and bitterness of chocolate, resulting in these bold, robust cupcakes.

INGREDIENTS

Chocolate Cupcake
Batter (see page 38),
with stout beer replacing
the heavy cream

FOR THE FILLING

1 cup (250 ml) stout beer,
slowly poured

1¼ teaspoons (2.5 g)
agar-agar powder

2 tablespoons (25 g) sugar

Chocolate buttercream
(see page 65)

Preheat the oven to 325°F on convection mode or 350°F for a conventional oven. Line three cupcake pans with paper liners.

Prepare the batter, transfer it to a piping bag, and pipe it into the paper liners. Place the cupcakes in the oven and bake until their internal temperature is 200°F, 20 to 25 minutes, rotating the pans halfway through.

Remove the cupcakes from the oven and let them rest in the pans for 5 minutes. Using an offset spatula, remove the cupcakes from the pans and transfer them to a cupcake holder. Cover them tightly and let them cool completely.

To begin preparations for the filling, place the stout in a small saucepan and bring it to a rapid boil. Combine the agar-agar powder and sugar in a bowl and then whisk the mixture into pan. Stir on medium heat until the stout has thickened, about 1 minute.

Transfer the mixture to a blender and puree on low until smooth. This is such a small quantity that blending on low will keep the gel toward the bottom of the beaker. If it's having difficulty coming together, stream in a bit more stout. Although it is a fluid gelatin, we do not want it to be too thin—just enough that it is pipable. Transfer the gelatin to a piping bag.

When the cupcakes are completely cool and ready to be frosted, prepare the buttercream.

Working from the tops of the cupcakes, remove their centers and fill them with the stout gelatin. Frost the cupcakes with the chocolate buttercream and serve.

Orange & Cardamom Cupcakes

YIELD: 36 CUPCAKES / **ACTIVE TIME:** 20 MINUTES / **TOTAL TIME:** 50 MINUTES

Cardamom has a complex flavor, with notes of citrus and a slightly floral undertone. In my opinion, it's the coziest of all the winter spices. It also pairs perfectly with oranges. Enjoy these by the fire the next time you're snowed in.

INGREDIENTS

FOR THE CUPCAKES

Butter Cupcake Batter (see page 36)

6 tablespoons (36 g) orange zest

2 teaspoons (5.2 g) cardamom

FOR THE FILLING

Milk Chocolate Ganache (see page 255), with Gran Gala liqueur replacing the bourbon

Pinch of cardamom

Big Fish Buttercream (see page 28)

Dehydrated Oranges (see page 261), for topping

Preheat the oven to 325°F on convection mode or 350°F for a conventional oven. Line three cupcake pans with paper liners.

To begin preparations for the cupcakes, prepare the batter, adding the orange zest after the eggs and the cardamom with the dry ingredients. Transfer it to a piping bag and pipe the batter into the paper liners.

Place the cupcakes in the oven and bake until their internal temperature is 200°F, 20 to 25 minutes, rotating the pans halfway through.

Remove the cupcakes from the oven and let them rest in the pans for 5 minutes. Using an offset spatula, remove the cupcakes from the pans and transfer them to a cupcake holder. Cover them tightly and let them cool completely.

Prepare the filling, adding the cardamom toward the end of the mixing process.

When the cupcakes are completely cool and ready to be frosted, prepare the buttercream.

Working from the tops of the cupcakes, remove their centers and fill them with the ganache. Frost the cupcakes with the buttercream, top them with Dehydrated Oranges, and serve.

Hazelnut Cupcakes

YIELD: 24 CUPCAKES / **ACTIVE TIME:** 20 MINUTES / **TOTAL TIME:** 50 MINUTES

I love how versatile hazelnuts are, how their nuttiness only enhances when roasted to a certain temperature, when baked in a batter, when candied. I'd be doing this book dirty if I didn't include a hazelnut cupcake for folks to enjoy.

INGREDIENTS

1 cup (220 g) brown sugar

½ cup (113 g) unsalted butter, softened

3 (174 g) eggs

1 cup (112 g) hazelnut flour

1 cup (125 g) all-purpose flour

2 teaspoons (9 g) baking powder

½ teaspoon (3 g) kosher salt

1 cup (230 g) sour cream

2 teaspoons (9 g) vanilla paste

Praline buttercream (see page 125)

Candied Hazelnuts (see page 261), for topping

Preheat the oven to 325°F on convection mode or 350°F for a conventional oven. Line two cupcake pans with paper liners.

Place the brown sugar and butter in the work bowl of a stand mixer fitted with the paddle attachment and beat until the mixture is light and fluffy, about 3 minutes. Scrape down the work bowl, add the eggs one at a time, and beat to incorporate.

Place the flours, baking powder, and salt in a bowl and whisk to combine. Sift the mixture through a fine-mesh tamis onto a piece of parchment paper. Fold the parchment paper lengthwise and add small increments of the dry mixture to the work bowl, beating to incorporate each addition and scraping down the work bowl as needed. Add the sour cream and vanilla and beat until the mixture comes together as a smooth batter.

Transfer it to a piping bag and pipe the batter into the paper liners. Place the cupcakes in the oven and bake until their internal temperature is 200°F, 20 to 25 minutes, rotating the pans halfway through.

Remove the cupcakes from the oven and let them rest in the pans for 5 minutes. Using an offset spatula, remove the cupcakes from the pans and transfer them to a cupcake holder. Cover them tightly and let them cool completely.

When the cupcakes are completely cool and ready to be frosted, prepare the buttercream.

Frost the cupcakes with the praline buttercream, top them with the Candied Hazelnuts, and serve.

Eggnog Cupcakes

YIELD: 24 CUPCAKES / ACTIVE TIME: 20 MINUTES / TOTAL TIME: 50 MINUTES

I love eggnog, but I can only drink maybe a cup a year, as it's too dense and fills me up before holiday feasts. Luckily, I've found that these cupcakes are a great alternative.

INGREDIENTS

1 cup (226 g) unsalted butter, melted

2 cups (400 g) sugar

4 (232 g) eggs

2 tablespoons (26 g) vanilla paste

¼ cup (50 ml) bourbon (optional)

3 cups (374 g) cake flour

1 tablespoon (14 g) baking powder

1 teaspoon (10 g) freshly grated nutmeg

½ teaspoon (3 g) kosher salt

1 cup (254 ml) eggnog

Butterscotch buttercream (see page 181)

Spiked Eggnog Ganache (see page 262), for filling

Preheat the oven to 325°F on convection mode or 350°F for a conventional oven. Line two cupcake pans with paper liners.

Place the butter, sugar, eggs, vanilla, and bourbon (if using) in a mixing bowl and whisk to combine.

Place the flour, baking powder, nutmeg, and salt in a bowl and whisk to combine. Sift the mixture through a fine-mesh tamis onto a piece of parchment paper. Fold the parchment paper lengthwise and alternate between adding small increments of the dry mixture and eggnog to the mixing bowl, folding to incorporate each addition and scraping down the mixing bowl as needed.

Transfer the batter to a piping bag and pipe it into the paper liners. Place the cupcakes in the oven and bake until their internal temperature is 200°F, 20 to 25 minutes, rotating the pans halfway through.

Remove the cupcakes from the oven and let them rest in the pans for 5 minutes. Using an offset spatula, remove the cupcakes from the pans and transfer them to a cupcake holder. Cover them tightly and let them cool completely.

When the cupcakes are completely cool and ready to be frosted, prepare the buttercream.

Working from the tops of the cupcakes, remove their centers and fill them with the ganache. Frost the cupcakes with the butterscotch buttercream and serve.

INGREDIENTS

1 lb. (454 g) unsalted butter

4 to 5 drops of fresh lemon juice

½ cup (125 g) sour cream

½ cup (120 ml) water

⅓ cup (90 g) egg whites

1 tablespoon (15 g) vanilla paste

1⅔ cups (205 g) all-purpose flour

1 cup (200 g) sugar

1½ teaspoons (6 g) baking powder

¼ teaspoon (2 g) baking soda

½ teaspoon (3 g) kosher salt

Butterscotch buttercream (see page 181)

Streusel (see page 254), for topping

Butterscotch Cupcakes

YIELD: 18 CUPCAKES / **ACTIVE TIME:** 20 MINUTES / **TOTAL TIME:** 50 MINUTES

I like to brown a whole pound of butter at a time, as that amount gives you more control over the process, and you can use what's left for so many things in your kitchen.

Preheat the oven to 325°F on convection mode or 350°F for a conventional oven. Line two cupcake pans with paper liners.

Place the butter in a small saucepan and melt it over medium heat. Once the butter has melted, the fats will start to separate and brown. As the fats separate, they will rise toward the surface; try to scoop them out with a small ladle so you can really see how brown your butter is getting. I've found that when the fats stop bubbling and foaming at the surface, the brown butter is closer to being done.

Tilt your pan to see the color of the butter closer to the bottom; you want it to be a light amber. It should also give off a nutty aroma; if it's not fragrant, keep browning the butter a bit longer.

Transfer the brown butter to a bowl and add the lemon juice; this stops the butter from cooking further. Let the brown butter cool for about 15 minutes.

Place ¾ cup of brown butter, the sour cream, water, egg whites, and vanilla in a mixing bowl and whisk to combine. Place the flour, sugar, baking powder, baking soda, and salt in a separate bowl and whisk to combine. Sift the mixture through a fine-mesh tamis onto a piece of parchment paper. Fold the parchment paper lengthwise, add the dry mixture to the wet mixture in small increments, and whisk until the resulting mixture comes together as a smooth batter.

Transfer the batter to a piping bag and pipe it into the paper liners. Place the cupcakes in the oven and bake until their internal temperature is 200°F, 20 to 25 minutes, rotating the pans halfway through.

Remove the cupcakes from the oven and let them rest in the pans for 5 minutes. Using an offset spatula, remove the cupcakes from the pans and transfer them to a cupcake holder. Cover them tightly and let them cool completely.

When the cupcakes are completely cool and ready to be frosted, prepare the buttercream.

Frost the cupcakes with the butterscotch buttercream, top them with Streusel, and serve.

Peanut Brittle Cupcakes

YIELD: 18 CUPCAKES / **ACTIVE TIME:** 20 MINUTES / **TOTAL TIME:** 50 MINUTES

I make brittle for my dad every Christmas, and he loves it so much that he jokes I should start a business just selling variations of the recipe. Despite not being a huge fan of peanut butter myself, I've discovered that it incorporates beautifully into the Big Fish Buttercream.

INGREDIENTS

Vanilla Cupcake Batter
(see page 34)

½ cup (113 g) Fabbri Caramel
Delipaste

Peanut butter buttercream
(see page 74)

Peanut Brittle (see page
262), for topping

Preheat the oven to 325°F on convection mode or 350°F for a conventional oven. Line two cupcake pans with paper liners.

Prepare the batter, adding the caramel before adding the dry mixture and heavy cream. Transfer it to a piping bag and pipe the batter into the paper liners.

Place the cupcakes in the oven and bake until their internal temperature is 200°F, 20 to 25 minutes, rotating the pans halfway through.

Remove the cupcakes from the oven and let them rest in the pans for 5 minutes. Using an offset spatula, remove the cupcakes from the pans and transfer them to a cupcake holder. Cover them tightly and let them cool completely.

When the cupcakes are completely cool and ready to be frosted, prepare the buttercream.

Frost the cupcakes with the peanut butter buttercream, top them with Peanut Brittle, and serve.

INGREDIENTS

FOR THE CUPCAKES

¼ cup (55 g) unsalted butter, softened

¾ cup (170 g) demerara sugar

1¼ cups (200 g) pitted fresh dates

1¼ cups (290 ml) boiling water

2 tablespoons (42 g) black treacle

1 tablespoon (24 g) golden syrup

2 (110 g) eggs

1⅔ cups (200 g) self-rising flour

1 tablespoon (13 g) baking soda

½ teaspoon (2 g) vanilla paste

FOR THE SAUCE

1 cup (220 ml) double cream

½ cup (110 g) unsalted butter

½ cup (110 g) brown sugar

¼ cup (84 g) black treacle

2 tablespoons (42 g) golden syrup

Whipped Cream
(see page 259)

Sticky Toffee Cupcakes

YIELD: 12 CUPCAKES / **ACTIVE TIME:** 30 MINUTES / **TOTAL TIME:** 1 HOUR

I'm throwing Derek some credit here, because this one is all him! He lived in England for five years while working as a pastry chef, and sticky toffee was a British classic that he grew to love and perfect. According to the man, the key here is using fresh dates, not dried. They can be slightly tricky to track down, so I try to call the shops in advance before searching for them myself. You can substitute molasses for black treacle, and corn syrup for golden syrup, but both of these beloved British ingredients can be purchased on Amazon and are a must for an authentic sticky toffee pudding.

Preheat the oven to 325°F on convection mode or 350°F for a conventional oven. Line a cupcake pan with paper liners.

To begin preparations for the cupcakes, place the butter and sugar in the work bowl of a stand mixer fitted with the paddle attachment and cream until the mixture is light and fluffy, about 3 minutes.

Place the dates and boiling water in a food processor and blitz until smooth.

With the stand mixer running, slowly stream in the black treacle and golden syrup and beat to incorporate. Add the eggs one at a time and beat to incorporate. Add the flour and beat to incorporate. Add the date puree, baking soda, and vanilla and beat until the mixture comes together as a smooth batter. Transfer it to a piping bag and pipe the batter into the paper liners.

Place the cupcakes in the oven and bake until their internal temperature is 200°F, 20 to 25 minutes, rotating the pan halfway through.

Remove the cupcakes from the oven and let them rest in the pan for 5 minutes. Using an offset spatula, remove the cupcakes from the pan and transfer them to a cupcake holder. Cover them tightly and let them cool completely.

When the cupcakes have completely cooled, prepare the sauce. Place all of the ingredients in a medium saucepan and bring to a boil, whisking until the sauce has emulsified.

Dip the tops of the cupcakes in the warm sauce, top them with Whipped Cream, and serve.

Pear & Ginger Cupcakes

YIELD: 18 CUPCAKES / **ACTIVE TIME:** 25 MINUTES / **TOTAL TIME:** 50 MINUTES

Personally, I would soften the pears in a pan with a pinch of sugar, vanilla, and a splash of your favorite brandy before letting them cool and adding them to the batter, but baking them raw is great too, as the juices will release and create a super-moist cupcake.

INGREDIENTS

FOR THE CUPCAKES

¾ cup (165 g) brown sugar

⅓ cup (73 g) canola oil

1 (55 g) egg

1 cup (244 ml) buttermilk

2½ cups (312 g) all-purpose flour

1 teaspoon (4.5 g) baking soda

2 teaspoon (5.5 g) ground ginger

½ teaspoon (3 g) kosher salt

1½ cups (210 g) chopped pears

FOR THE BUTTERCREAM

Italian Meringue Buttercream (see page 29)

¼ cup (24 g) ground ginger

Preheat the oven to 325°F on convection mode or 350°F for a conventional oven. Line two cupcake pans with paper liners.

To begin preparations for the cupcakes, place the brown sugar, canola oil, egg, and buttermilk in a mixing bowl and stir to combine. Sift the flour into a separate mixing bowl, add the baking soda, ginger, and salt, and whisk to combine. Sift the dry mixture through a fine-mesh tamis onto a piece of parchment paper. Fold the parchment paper lengthwise, add the dry mixture to the wet mixture in small increments, and fold until the resulting mixture comes together as a smooth batter. Add the pears and fold to incorporate.

Transfer the batter to a piping bag and pipe it into the paper liners. Place the cupcakes in the oven and bake until their internal temperature is 200°F, 20 to 25 minutes, rotating the pans halfway through.

Remove the cupcakes from the oven and let them rest in the pans for 5 minutes. Using an offset spatula, remove the cupcakes from the pans and transfer them to a cupcake holder. Cover them tightly and let them cool completely.

When the cupcakes have completely cooled and are ready to be frosted, prepare the Italian Meringue Buttercream. Add the ginger and beat to incorporate.

Frost the cupcakes with the ginger buttercream and serve.

Peppermint Cupcakes

YIELD: 24 CUPCAKES / **ACTIVE TIME:** 25 MINUTES / **TOTAL TIME:** 50 MINUTES

Perfect for a holiday get-together, as they pair so well with dessert cocktails, and will match everyone's outfit.

INGREDIENTS

FOR THE CUPCAKES

Chocolate Cupcake Batter
(see page 38)

2½ teaspoons (9 ml) LorAnn
Peppermint Oil

FOR THE BUTTERCREAM

Big Fish Buttercream
(see page 28)

1 tablespoon (13 ml) LorAnn
Peppermint Oil

Preheat the oven to 325°F on convection mode or 350°F for a conventional oven. Line two cupcake pans with paper liners.

To begin preparations for the cupcakes, prepare the batter, adding the peppermint oil toward the end of the mixing process.

Transfer the batter to a piping bag and pipe it into the paper liners. Place the cupcakes in the oven and bake until their internal temperature is 200°F, 20 to 25 minutes, rotating the pans halfway through.

Remove the cupcakes from the oven and let them rest in the pans for 5 minutes. Using an offset spatula, remove the cupcakes from the pans and transfer them to a cupcake holder. Cover them tightly and let them cool completely.

When the cupcakes have completely cooled and are ready to be frosted, prepare the Big Fish Buttercream. Add the peppermint oil and beat to incorporate.

Frost the cupcakes with the peppermint buttercream and serve.

HOLIDAYS

*T*he expressive ability of cupcakes creates numerous moments where they can capture the desired vibe, but around the holidays they become imbued with particularly special powers, able to produce the buzz of joy that we are after during these occasions, and set these holiday celebrations down in everyone's minds as can't-miss affairs.

New Year's Eve Cupcakes

YIELD: 24 CUPCAKES / ACTIVE TIME: 20 MINUTES / TOTAL TIME: 50 MINUTES

Hosting an NYE party? Pass these around with the Champagne to elevate and sweeten your midnight toast.

INGREDIENTS

Champagne cupcake batter
(see page 46)

Big Fish Buttercream
(see page 28)

Preheat the oven to 325°F on convection mode or 350°F for a conventional oven. Line two cupcake pans with paper liners.

Prepare the batter, transfer it to a piping bag, and pipe it into the paper liners. Place the cupcakes in the oven and bake until their internal temperature is 200°F, 20 to 25 minutes, rotating the pans halfway through.

Remove the cupcakes from the oven and let them rest in the pans for 5 minutes. Using an offset spatula, remove the cupcakes from the pans and transfer them to a cupcake holder. Cover them tightly and let them cool completely.

When the cupcakes have completely cooled and are ready to be frosted, prepare the buttercream.

Frost the cupcakes with the buttercream and serve.

Valentine's Day Cupcakes

YIELD: 36 CUPCAKES / **ACTIVE TIME:** 20 MINUTES / **TOTAL TIME:** 50 MINUTES

Who says you have to choose between cupcakes and chocolate strawberries on Valentine's Day? Not I. Make these and enjoy a stay-in date night this V-Day, avoiding the crowds and the exorbitant prices.

INGREDIENTS

Red velvet cupcake batter
(see page 57)

Strawberry buttercream
(see page 147)

Preheat the oven to 325°F on convection mode or 350°F for a conventional oven. Line three cupcake pans with paper liners.

Prepare the batter, transfer it to a piping bag, and pipe it into the paper liners. Place the cupcakes in the oven and bake until their internal temperature is 200°F, 20 to 25 minutes, rotating the pans halfway through.

Remove the cupcakes from the oven and let them rest in the pans for 5 minutes. Using an offset spatula, remove the cupcakes from the pans and transfer them to a cupcake holder. Cover them tightly and let them cool completely.

When the cupcakes have completely cooled and are ready to be frosted, prepare the buttercream.

Frost the cupcakes with the strawberry buttercream and serve.

St. Patrick's Day Cupcakes

YIELD: 30 CUPCAKES / **ACTIVE TIME:** 20 MINUTES / **TOTAL TIME:** 45 MINUTES

Kiss me, I'm Irish. In addition to having a little fun, I've infused this cupcake with the velvety quality of an Irish Coffee, making it a true delight.

INGREDIENTS

Chocolate Cupcake Batter (see page 38), with Baileys Irish Cream replacing the milk

Espresso buttercream (see page 85)

Milk Chocolate Ganache (see page 255), with Irish whiskey replacing the bourbon, for filling

Preheat the oven to 325°F on convection mode or 350°F for a conventional oven. Line three cupcake pans with paper liners.

Prepare the batter, transfer it to a piping bag, and pipe it into the paper liners. Place the cupcakes in the oven and bake until their internal temperature is 200°F, 20 to 25 minutes, rotating the pans halfway through.

Remove the cupcakes from the oven and let them rest in the pans for 5 minutes. Using an offset spatula, remove the cupcakes from the pans and transfer them to a cupcake holder. Cover them tightly and let them cool completely.

When the cupcakes have completely cooled and are ready to be frosted, prepare the buttercream.

Working from the tops of the cupcakes, remove their centers and fill them with the ganache. Frost the cupcakes with the espresso buttercream and serve.

Mother's Day Cupcakes

YIELD: 24 CUPCAKES / **ACTIVE TIME:** 20 MINUTES / **TOTAL TIME:** 50 MINUTES

Before making these for your own mother, ask yourself, What's Mom's favorite tea? You can easily substitute chamomile, jasmine, or any tea that pairs well with citrus and honey for the Earl Grey in the batter. Make the buttercream her favorite color, and voilà, you have a yummy way to show Mom your appreciation this Mother's Day.

INGREDIENTS

Earl Grey cupcake batter (see page 73)

¾ sheet (1.9 g) of silver gelatin

½ cup (108 g) Boiron bergamot puree

2 (108 g) eggs

½ cup (108 g) sugar

9¾ tablespoons (140 g) unsalted butter, softened

Honey buttercream (see page 49)

Preheat the oven to 325°F on convection mode or 350°F for a conventional oven. Line two cupcake pans with paper liners.

Prepare the batter, transfer it to a piping bag, and pipe it into the paper liners. Place the cupcakes in the oven and bake until their internal temperature is 200°F, 20 to 25 minutes, rotating the pans halfway through.

Remove the cupcakes from the oven and let them rest in the pans for 5 minutes. Using an offset spatula, remove the cupcakes from the pans and transfer them to a cupcake holder. Cover them tightly and let them cool completely.

Place the gelatin in a bowl of water and let it bloom. Place the bergamot puree, eggs, and sugar in a small saucepan and warm the mixture over medium heat, whisking continually, until it reaches 170°F and starts to thicken. Strain the mixture into a blender, add the bloomed gelatin and butter, and puree until smooth. Transfer the curd to a small bowl and place plastic wrap directly on the surface to prevent a skin from forming. Let the curd cool completely.

When the cupcakes have completely cooled and are ready to be frosted, prepare the buttercream.

Working from the tops of the cupcakes, remove their centers and fill them with the curd. Frost the cupcakes with the honey buttercream and serve.

Father's Day Cupcakes

YIELD: 30 CUPCAKES / **ACTIVE TIME:** 20 MINUTES / **TOTAL TIME:** 45 MINUTES

If your dad doesn't dance while grilling dogs in a business suit, drinking a glass of Scotch, and rocking a mustache, is he even a dad? Is that just my dad? Shout-out to you, Eugene, the only man I will bake chocolate-and-peanut-butter anything for.

INGREDIENTS

Chocolate Cupcake Batter
(see page 38)

Peanut butter buttercream
(see page 74)

Preheat the oven to 325°F on convection mode or 350°F for a conventional oven. Line three cupcake pans with paper liners.

Prepare the batter, transfer it to a piping bag, and pipe it into the paper liners. Place the cupcakes in the oven and bake until their internal temperature is 200°F, 20 to 25 minutes, rotating the pans halfway through.

Remove the cupcakes from the oven and let them rest in the pans for 5 minutes. Using an offset spatula, remove the cupcakes from the pans and transfer them to a cupcake holder. Cover them tightly and let them cool completely.

When the cupcakes have completely cooled and are ready to be frosted, prepare the buttercream.

Frost the cupcakes with the peanut butter buttercream and serve.

Earth Day Cupcakes

YIELD: 24 CUPCAKES / ACTIVE TIME: 25 MINUTES / TOTAL TIME: 50 MINUTES

This unique creation blends the earthy sweetness of parsnips with the richness of brown butter, creating a flavor that celebrates the bountiful gifts nature supplies. To take these to a deeper, savory level, add 1 to 2 tablespoons of chopped fresh thyme to the batter.

INGREDIENTS

½ cup (113 g) brown butter (see page 203)

½ cup (110 g) brown sugar

½ cup (100 g) sugar

Zest of 1 orange

2 (110 g) eggs

2 teaspoons (8.5 g) vanilla paste

½ teaspoon (2.5 ml) almond extract

1 cup (120 g) cake flour

¾ cup (90 g) all-purpose flour

⅓ cup (30 g) almond flour

½ teaspoon (2 g) baking powder

1 teaspoon (6 g) baking soda

2 teaspoons (12 g) kosher salt

1 tablespoon (6.5 g) Spice Girl Mix (see page 254)

½ cup (95 g) yogurt

2 cups (244 g) peeled and shredded parsnips

Honey buttercream (see page 49)

Preheat the oven to 325°F on convection mode or 350°F for a conventional oven. Line two cupcake pans with paper liners.

Place the brown butter, brown sugar, sugar, and orange zest in the work bowl of a stand mixer fitted with the paddle attachment and cream until the mixture is pale and fluffy, 3 to 5 minutes. Scrape down the work bowl, add the eggs one at a time, and beat to incorporate. Add the vanilla and almond extract and beat to incorporate.

Place the flours, baking powder, baking soda, salt, and Spice Girl Mix in a bowl and whisk to combine. Sift the mixture through a fine-mesh tamis onto a piece of parchment paper. Fold the parchment paper lengthwise. With the mixer running on low, alternate between adding small increments of the dry mixture and yogurt to the work bowl, scraping down the work bowl as needed. Add the parsnips and fold until they are evenly distributed.

Transfer the batter to a piping bag and pipe it into the paper liners.

Place the cupcakes in the oven and bake until their internal temperature is 200°F, 20 to 25 minutes, rotating the pans halfway through.

Remove the cupcakes from the oven and let them rest in the pans for 5 minutes. Using an offset spatula, remove the cupcakes from the pans and transfer them to a cupcake holder. Cover them tightly and let them cool completely.

When the cupcakes have cooled completely and are ready to be frosted, prepare the buttercream.

Frost the cupcakes with the honey buttercream and serve.

Pride Day Cupcakes

YIELD: 36 CUPCAKES / **ACTIVE TIME:** 20 MINUTES / **TOTAL TIME:** 50 MINUTES

Never apologize for who you are, who you love, or when you make a mess decorating.

INGREDIENTS

Funfetti cupcake batter
(see page 54)

Italian Meringue
Buttercream (see page 29)

Preheat the oven to 325°F on convection mode or 350°F for a conventional oven. Line three cupcake pans with paper liners.

Prepare the batter, transfer it to a piping bag, and pipe it into the paper liners. Place the cupcakes in the oven and bake until their internal temperature is 200°F, 20 to 25 minutes, rotating the pans halfway through.

Remove the cupcakes from the oven and let them rest in the pans for 5 minutes. Using an offset spatula, remove the cupcakes from the pans and transfer them to a cupcake holder. Cover them tightly and let them cool completely.

When the cupcakes have completely cooled and are ready to be frosted, prepare the buttercream.

Frost the cupcakes with the buttercream and serve.

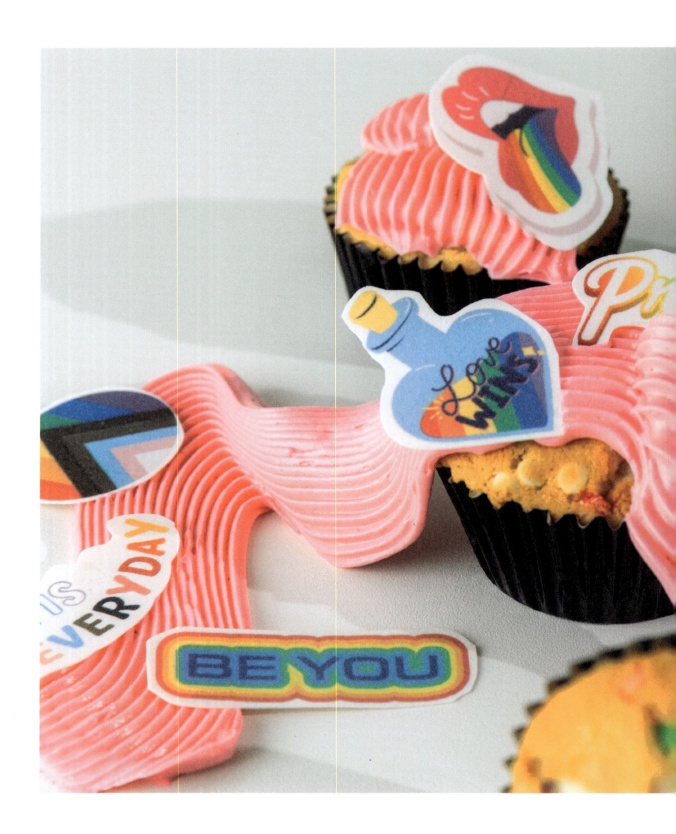

PRIDE DAY CUPCAKES, SEE PAGE 225

Halloween Cupcakes

YIELD: 30 CUPCAKES / **ACTIVE TIME:** 20 MINUTES / **TOTAL TIME:** 45 MINUTES

Sink your fangs into a moist chocolate cupcake that is as dark as the night. Print your favorite spooky image on some fondant, match your buttercream to it, and consider filling the inside with your favorite Halloween candy. So many spooky possibilities to play with here.

INGREDIENTS

FOR THE CUPCAKES

Chocolate Cupcake Batter (see page 38)

1 tablespoon (6.5 g) Spice Girl Mix (see page 254)

2 tablespoons (27 ml) maple extract

FOR THE BUTTERCREAM

White chocolate buttercream (see page 42)

1 tablespoon (13 ml) maple extract

Preheat the oven to 325°F on convection mode or 350°F for a conventional oven. Line three cupcake pans with paper liners.

To begin preparations for the cupcakes, prepare the batter, adding the Spice Girl Mix with the dry ingredients and the maple extract toward the end of the mixing process.

Transfer the batter to a piping bag and pipe it into the paper liners. Place the cupcakes in the oven and bake until their internal temperature is 200°F, 20 to 25 minutes, rotating the pans halfway through.

Remove the cupcakes from the oven and let them rest in the pans for 5 minutes. Using an offset spatula, remove the cupcakes from the pans and transfer them to a cupcake holder. Cover them tightly and let them cool completely.

When the cupcakes have completely cooled and are ready to be frosted, prepare the white chocolate buttercream. Add the maple extract and beat to incorporate.

Frost the cupcakes with the white chocolate and maple buttercream and serve.

Thanksgiving Cupcakes

YIELD: 30 CUPCAKES / **ACTIVE TIME:** 20 MINUTES / **TOTAL TIME:** 45 MINUTES

You can make a cupcake look like a pie, but can you make a pie look like a cupcake? Debatable. I have made many different confections based on the flavors of traditional T-Day desserts, but I think these were the most fun.

INGREDIENTS

Pumpkin spice cupcake batter (see page 189)

120 to 150 fresh cranberries

Ginger buttercream (see page 208)

Preheat the oven to 325°F on convection mode or 350°F for a conventional oven. Line three cupcake pans with paper liners.

Prepare the batter, transfer it to a piping bag, and pipe it into the paper liners. Top each cupcake with 4 to 5 cranberries. Place the cupcakes in the oven and bake until their internal temperature is 200°F, 20 to 25 minutes, rotating the pans halfway through.

Remove the cupcakes from the oven and let them rest in the pans for 5 minutes. Using an offset spatula, remove the cupcakes from the pans and transfer them to a cupcake holder. Cover them tightly and let them cool completely.

When the cupcakes have completely cooled and are ready to be frosted, prepare the buttercream.

Frost the cupcakes with the ginger buttercream and serve.

4th of July Cupcakes

YIELD: 36 CUPCAKES / **ACTIVE TIME:** 20 MINUTES / **TOTAL TIME:** 50 MINUTES

The 4th makes most people think of fireworks, but I think of racing to the ice cream truck for a rocket bomb pop.

INGREDIENTS

Vanilla Cupcake Batter
(see page 34)

Grenadine buttercream
(see page 169)

Preheat the oven to 325°F on convection mode or 350°F for a conventional oven. Line three cupcake pans with paper liners.

Prepare the batter, transfer it to a piping bag, and pipe it into the paper liners. Place the cupcakes in the oven and bake until their internal temperature is 200°F, 20 to 25 minutes, rotating the pans halfway through.

Remove the cupcakes from the oven and let them rest in the pans for 5 minutes. Using an offset spatula, remove the cupcakes from the pans and transfer them to a cupcake holder. Cover them tightly and let them cool completely.

When the cupcakes have completely cooled and are ready to be frosted, prepare the buttercream.

Frost the cupcakes with the grenadine buttercream and serve.

4TH OF JULY CUPCAKES, SEE PAGE 231

Christmas Cupcakes

YIELD: 24 CUPCAKES / **ACTIVE TIME:** 20 MINUTES / **TOTAL TIME:** 45 MINUTES

Filled with a silky, spicy ganache, these cupcakes are way more exciting than the traditional gingerbread men—you're welcome, Santa.

INGREDIENTS

1 cup (227 g) unsalted butter, softened

1½ cups (330 g) brown sugar

1½ cups (505 g) molasses

2 teaspoons (8 g) vanilla paste

2 (110 g) eggs

4 cups (500 g) all-purpose flour

1 tablespoon (13 g) baking soda

1 teaspoon (6 g) kosher salt

2 tablespoons (15 g) Spice Girl Mix (see page 254)

2 cups (473 ml) boiling water

Orange and cranberry buttercream (see page 183)

Gingerbread Ganache (see page 261), for filling

Preheat the oven to 325°F on convection mode or 350°F for a conventional oven. Line two cupcake pans with paper liners.

Place the butter and brown sugar in the work bowl of a stand mixer fitted with the paddle attachment and cream until the mixture is pale and fluffy, 3 to 5 minutes. Scrape down the work bowl, add the molasses and vanilla, and beat to incorporate. Scrape down the work bowl, add the eggs one at a time, and beat to incorporate.

Place the flour, baking soda, salt, and Spice Girl Mix in a bowl and whisk to combine. Sift the mixture through a fine-mesh tamis onto a piece of parchment paper. Fold the parchment paper lengthwise, add small increments of the dry mixture to the work bowl, and beat to combine, scraping down the work bowl as needed. With the mixer running on low, slowly stream in the boiling water.

Transfer the batter to a piping bag and pipe it into the paper liners.

Place the cupcakes in the oven and bake until their internal temperature is 200°F, 20 to 25 minutes, rotating the pans halfway through.

Remove the cupcakes from the oven and let them rest in the pans for 5 minutes. Using an offset spatula, remove the cupcakes from the pans and transfer them to a cupcake holder. Cover them tightly and let them cool completely.

When the cupcakes have cooled completely and are ready to be frosted, prepare the buttercream.

Working from the tops of the cupcakes, remove their centers and fill them with the ganache. Frost the cupcakes with the orange and cranberry buttercream and serve.

FOR THE KIDS

*S*ure, kids love sweets. But they also like those sweets to take certain forms—sugary, straightforward, freighted with familiar flavors, and eye-catching. These recipes check every single one of those boxes, letting your little ones feel the immense love you have for them, and you to bask in the smiles on their faces.

Funfetti Cupcakes

YIELD: 36 CUPCAKES / **ACTIVE TIME:** 20 MINUTES / **TOTAL TIME:** 50 MINUTES

Have you ever made America's favorite cake flavor from scratch? I tested this batter with many different sprinkles, thinking the finer, more modern sprinkles would do the trick. Nope, the common round, overly sweet sprinkles are what gives Funfetti its unique flavor.

INGREDIENTS

Funfetti cupcake batter
(see page 54)

Swiss Meringue
Buttercream (see page 31)

Preheat the oven to 325°F on convection mode or 350°F for a conventional oven. Line three cupcake pans with paper liners.

Prepare the batter, transfer it to a piping bag, and pipe it into the paper liners. Place the cupcakes in the oven and bake until their internal temperature is 200°F, 20 to 25 minutes, rotating the pans halfway through.

Remove the cupcakes from the oven and let them rest in the pans for 5 minutes. Using an offset spatula, remove the cupcakes from the pans and transfer them to a cupcake holder. Cover them tightly and let them cool completely.

When the cupcakes have completely cooled and are ready to be frosted, prepare the buttercream.

Frost the cupcakes with the buttercream and serve.

Cookie Dough Cupcakes

YIELD: 36 CUPCAKES / **ACTIVE TIME:** 20 MINUTES / **TOTAL TIME:** 50 MINUTES

Since kids change their minds so often, it can be a challenge letting them pick the flavor of their birthday cake. If you're looking for a flavor that's sure to be a hit, consider mentioning this cookie dough frosting as a possibility—it'll blow their mind.

INGREDIENTS

FOR THE CUPCAKES

Vanilla Cupcake Batter (see page 34)

¾ cup (116 g) chocolate chips

All-purpose flour, as needed

FOR THE FROSTING

6 tablespoons (82 g) brown sugar

¼ cup (56 g) unsalted butter, softened

½ cup (55 g) all-purpose flour, plus more as needed

¼ teaspoon (1.5 g) kosher salt

½ teaspoon (2 g) vanilla paste

2 tablespoons (30 ml) milk

¼ cup (42 g) mini chocolate chips

Preheat the oven to 325°F on convection mode or 350°F for a conventional oven. Line three cupcake pans with paper liners.

To begin preparations for the cupcakes, prepare the batter. Place the chocolate chips in a mixing bowl, sprinkle flour over them, and toss to coat. Add the chocolate chips to the batter and fold until they are evenly distributed.

Transfer the batter to a piping bag and pipe it into the paper liners. Place the cupcakes in the oven and bake until their internal temperature is 200°F, 20 to 25 minutes, rotating the pans halfway through.

Remove the cupcakes from the oven and let them rest in the pans for 5 minutes. Using an offset spatula, remove the cupcakes from the pans and transfer them to a cupcake holder. Cover them tightly and let them cool completely.

When the cupcakes have completely cooled and are ready to be frosted, prepare the frosting. Place the brown sugar and butter in the work bowl of a stand mixer fitted with the paddle attachment and cream until the mixture is light and fluffy, about 5 minutes. Add the flour, salt, vanilla, and milk and beat to incorporate. Add the mini chocolate chips and fold until they are evenly distributed.

Frost the cupcakes with the cookie dough frosting and serve.

Banana Split Cupcakes

YIELD: 36 CUPCAKES / **ACTIVE TIME:** 20 MINUTES / **TOTAL TIME:** 50 MINUTES

Please, if you take one piece of advice from this book, serve these with a scoop of ice cream.

INGREDIENTS

8 (907 g) bananas, peeled

½ cup (113 ml) heavy cream

½ cup (115 g) crème fraîche

2⅛ cups (454 g) sugar

4 (220 g) eggs

½ cup (113 ml) canola oil

4⅓ cups (538 g) all-purpose flour

1¾ tablespoons (24 g) baking powder

Italian Meringue Buttercream (see page 29)

Preheat the oven to 325°F on convection mode or 350°F for a conventional oven. Line three cupcake pans with paper liners.

Place the bananas, heavy cream, and crème fraîche in the work bowl of a stand mixer fitted with the paddle attachment and beat to combine, 1 to 2 minutes. Add the sugar and beat to incorporate. Add the eggs and canola oil and beat for 1 minute.

Place the flour and baking powder in a mixing bowl and whisk to combine. Sift the mixture through a fine-mesh tamis onto a piece of parchment paper. Fold the parchment paper lengthwise. Scrape down the work bowl and add small increments of the dry mixture to the work bowl, beating to incorporate.

Transfer the batter to a piping bag and pipe it into the paper liners. Place the cupcakes in the oven and bake until their internal temperature is 200°F, 20 to 25 minutes, rotating the pans halfway through.

Remove the cupcakes from the oven and let them rest in the pans for 5 minutes. Using an offset spatula, remove the cupcakes from the pans and transfer them to a cupcake holder. Cover them tightly and let them cool completely.

When the cupcakes have completely cooled and are ready to be frosted, prepare the buttercream.

Frost the cupcakes with the buttercream and serve.

BANANA SPLIT CUPCAKES, SEE PAGE 241

Cookies & Cream Cupcakes

YIELD: 36 CUPCAKES / **ACTIVE TIME:** 20 MINUTES / **TOTAL TIME:** 50 MINUTES

I grew up in New England, and being a summer baby, I had a Friendly's ice cream cake every year, the one with the irresistible chocolate crumble between the layers of ice cream. This Chocolate Soil is my version of that crumble.

INGREDIENTS

Marble cupcake batter (see page 65)

Big Fish Buttercream (see page 28)

Chocolate Soil (see page 262), for filling

Preheat the oven to 325°F on convection mode or 350°F for a conventional oven. Line three cupcake pans with paper liners.

Prepare the batter, transfer it to a piping bag, and pipe it into the paper liners. Place the cupcakes in the oven and bake until their internal temperature is 200°F, 20 to 25 minutes, rotating the pans halfway through.

Remove the cupcakes from the oven and let them rest in the pans for 5 minutes. Using an offset spatula, remove the cupcakes from the pans and transfer them to a cupcake holder. Cover them tightly and let them cool completely.

When the cupcakes have completely cooled and are ready to be frosted, prepare the buttercream.

Working from the tops of the cupcakes, remove their centers and fill them with the Chocolate Soil. Frost the cupcakes with the buttercream and serve.

Neapolitan Cupcakes

YIELD: 36 CUPCAKES / **ACTIVE TIME:** 20 MINUTES / **TOTAL TIME:** 50 MINUTES

Tell the kids you're going to have an ice cream party and then bake these fun ice cream cupcakes! Base them around your family's favorite ice cream flavors and build your own "sundae."

INGREDIENTS

Vanilla Cupcake Batter
(see page 34)

Chocolate Cupcake Batter
(see page 38)

Strawberry Cupcake Batter
(see page 131)

Big Fish Buttercream
(see page 28)

Chocolate buttercream
(see page 65)

Strawberry buttercream
(see page 147)

Preheat the oven to 325°F on convection mode or 350°F for a conventional oven. Line three cupcake pans with paper liners.

Prepare the batters, transfer each one to its own piping bag, and pipe them into the paper liners. Place the cupcakes in the oven and bake until their internal temperature is 200°F, 20 to 25 minutes, rotating the pans halfway through.

Remove the cupcakes from the oven and let them rest in the pans for 5 minutes. Using an offset spatula, remove the cupcakes from the pans and transfer them to a cupcake holder. Cover them tightly and let them cool completely.

When the cupcakes have completely cooled and are ready to be frosted, prepare the buttercreams.

Frost the cupcakes with the buttercreams and serve.

NEAPOLITAN CUPCAKES, SEE PAGE 245

Peanut Butter & Jelly Cupcakes

YIELD: 24 CUPCAKES / **ACTIVE TIME:** 20 MINUTES / **TOTAL TIME:** 50 MINUTES

Perfect for kids and kids at heart, these cupcakes are a playful treat that never goes out of style.

INGREDIENTS

⅓ cup (80 g) unsalted butter

⅓ cup (75 ml) canola oil

½ cup (100 g) sugar

¾ cup (165 g) brown sugar

⅔ cup (172 g) creamy peanut butter

3 (165 g) eggs

1½ teaspoons (6 g) vanilla paste

1⅔ cups (210 g) all-purpose flour

3 tablespoons (24 g) cornstarch

½ teaspoon (2 g) baking soda

2 teaspoons (9 g) baking powder

½ teaspoon (2 g) kosher salt

1 cup (225 ml) buttermilk

Peanut butter buttercream (see page 74)

Mixed Berry Compote (see page 255), for filling

Preheat the oven to 325°F on convection mode or 350°F in a conventional oven. Line two cupcake pans with paper liners.

Place the butter, canola oil, sugar, brown sugar, and peanut butter in the work bowl of a stand mixer fitted with the paddle attachment and beat until the mixture is light and fluffy, 3 to 5 minutes. Scrape down the work bowl, add the eggs one at a time, and beat to incorporate. Add the vanilla and beat to incorporate.

Place the flour, cornstarch, baking soda, baking powder, and salt in a bowl and whisk to combine. Sift the mixture through a fine-mesh tamis onto a piece of parchment paper. Fold the parchment paper lengthwise and alternate between adding small increments of the dry mixture and buttermilk to the work bowl, beating to incorporate each addition and scraping down the work bowl as needed.

Transfer the batter to a piping bag, pipe it into the paper liners, and place the cupcakes in the oven. Bake until their internal temperature is 200°F, 20 to 25 minutes, rotating the pans halfway through.

Remove the cupcakes from the oven and let them rest in the pans for 5 minutes. Using an offset spatula, remove the cupcakes from the pans and transfer them to a cupcake holder. Cover them tightly and let them cool completely.

When the cupcakes have completely cooled and are ready to be frosted, prepare the buttercream.

Working from the tops of the cupcakes, remove their centers and fill them with the compote. Frost the cupcakes with the peanut butter buttercream and serve.

Candy Cupcakes

YIELD: 24 CUPCAKES / **ACTIVE TIME:** 20 MINUTES / **TOTAL TIME:** 50 MINUTES

These are for all those whose sweet tooth isn't satisfied unless something that matches the sweetness of candy is involved.

INGREDIENTS

Red velvet cupcake batter (see page 57)

Big Fish Buttercream (see page 28)

1 teaspoon (5 ml) LorAnn Green Apple Flavoring Extract

1 teaspoon (5 ml) LorAnn Tart & Sour Flavor Enhancer

1 teaspoon (5 ml) LorAnn Bubble Gum Flavoring Extract

Preheat the oven to 325°F on convection mode or 350°F for a conventional oven. Line two cupcake pans with paper liners.

Prepare the batter, transfer it to a piping bag, and pipe it into the paper liners. Place the cupcakes in the oven and bake until their internal temperature is 200°F, 20 to 25 minutes, rotating the pans halfway through.

Remove the cupcakes from the oven and let them rest in the pans for 5 minutes. Using an offset spatula, remove the cupcakes from the pans and transfer them to a cupcake holder. Cover them tightly and let them cool completely.

When the cupcakes have completely cooled and are ready to be frosted, prepare the buttercream. Place half of the buttercream in a separate bowl. Add the green apple extract and tart & sour enhancer to one portion and stir to incorporate. Add the bubble gum extract to the other portion and stir to incorporate.

Frost the cupcakes with the buttercreams and serve.

Cotton Candy Cupcakes

YIELD: 24 CUPCAKES / **ACTIVE TIME:** 20 MINUTES / **TOTAL TIME:** 50 MINUTES

These cupcakes are a feast for the eyes and taste buds alike. The cotton candy topping shown in the photo is not essential, but it certainly takes these cupcakes to another level.

INGREDIENTS

Strawberry cupcake batter
(see page 131)

Big Fish Buttercream
(see page 28)

LorAnn Cotton Candy
Flavoring Extract, to taste

LorAnn Blue Raspberry
Flavoring Extract, to taste

Preheat the oven to 325°F on convection mode or 350°F for a conventional oven. Line two cupcake pans with paper liners.

Prepare the batter, transfer it to a piping bag, and pipe it into the paper liners. Place the cupcakes in the oven and bake until their internal temperature is 200°F, 20 to 25 minutes, rotating the pans halfway through.

Remove the cupcakes from the oven and let them rest in the pans for 5 minutes. Using an offset spatula, remove the cupcakes from the pans and transfer them to a cupcake holder. Cover them tightly and let them cool completely.

When the cupcakes have completely cooled and are ready to be frosted, prepare the buttercream. Place half of the buttercream in a separate bowl. Add cotton candy extract to one portion and stir to incorporate. Add blue raspberry extract to the other portion and stir to incorporate.

Frost the cupcakes with the buttercreams and serve.

Appendix

INGREDIENTS

½ cup cinnamon

¼ cup ground ginger

¼ cup cardamom

2 tablespoons ground cloves

2 tablespoons freshly grated nutmeg

SPICE GIRL MIX

YIELD: 1¼ CUPS / **ACTIVE TIME:** 10 MINUTES / **TOTAL TIME:** 10 MINUTES

Place all of the ingredients in an airtight container, cover it, and shake to combine. Use as desired.

INGREDIENTS

1½ cups fresh blueberries

⅓ cup sugar

Zest and juice of 1 lemon

BLUEBERRY COMPOTE

YIELD: 1 CUP / **ACTIVE TIME:** 20 MINUTES / **TOTAL TIME:** 1 HOUR

Place all of the ingredients in a small saucepan and warm over medium heat, stirring occasionally, until the berries have softened, about 10 minutes.

Strain the berries, reserving all of the juices. Set the berries aside.

Add the juices back to the pan and cook over medium heat until they have reduced by half, taking care not to let the juices burn.

Remove the pan from heat and let the juices cool to room temperature.

Fold in the berries and use as desired.

INGREDIENTS

2 cups gluten-free flour

1 cup brown sugar

½ cup sugar

2 teaspoons kosher salt

2¾ tablespoons Spice Girl Mix (see page 254)

1 cup unsalted butter, chilled

STREUSEL

YIELD: 6 CUPS / **ACTIVE TIME:** 20 MINUTES / **TOTAL TIME:** 50 MINUTES

Preheat the oven to 325°F on convection mode or 350°F for a conventional oven. Line a baking sheet with a Silpat mat.

Combine all of the ingredients, except for the butter, in the work bowl of a stand mixer fitted with the paddle attachment.

Dice the butter into small cubes. With the mixer running, add the butter and beat until the mixture has a sandy, crumbly texture. Spread the mixture over the Silpat mat and place it in the freezer for 20 minutes.

Remove the baking sheet from the freezer, place it in the oven, and bake until the streusel is golden brown, about 20 minutes.

Remove the streusel from the oven and let it cool to room temperature.

Place the streusel in a food processor and pulse until it is small, sandy chunks. Use as desired.

INGREDIENTS

½ cup cacao nibs

½ cup dark chocolate chips

CACAO NIB CRUMB

YIELD: 1 CUP / **ACTIVE TIME:** 10 MINUTES / **TOTAL TIME:** 10 MINUTES

Place all of the ingredients in a food processor and pulse until the mixture is fine. Use as desired.

MILK CHOCOLATE GANACHE

YIELD: 2 CUPS / **ACTIVE TIME:** 10 MINUTES / **TOTAL TIME:** 20 MINUTES

INGREDIENTS

⅔ cup heavy cream

2 tablespoons glucose

1¾ cups milk chocolate

2 tablespoons bourbon

Place the heavy cream and glucose in a small saucepan and bring to a boil.

Place the chocolate in a heatproof bowl and pour the cream mixture over it. Let it sit for 30 seconds and then stir until the mixture is smooth, adding more heat if necessary.

Add the bourbon and stir to incorporate it. Let the ganache cool just enough that it won't melt a buttercream but can still be piped into cupcakes and use as desired.

MIXED BERRY COMPOTE

YIELD: 2 CUPS / **ACTIVE TIME:** 20 MINUTES / **TOTAL TIME:** 1 HOUR

INGREDIENTS

2½ cups frozen mixed berries

¾ cup sugar

Zest and juice of 1 lemon

Place all of the ingredients in a small saucepan and warm over medium heat, stirring occasionally, until the berries have softened, about 10 minutes.

Strain the berries, reserving all of the juices. Set the berries aside.

Add the juices back to the pan and cook over medium heat until they have reduced by half, taking care not to let the juices burn.

Remove the pan from heat and let the juices cool to room temperature.

Fold in the berries and use as desired.

DULCE DE LECHE

YIELD: 1 CUP / **ACTIVE TIME:** 20 MINUTES

TOTAL TIME: 3 HOURS AND 30 MINUTES

INGREDIENTS

1 (14 oz.) can of sweetened condensed milk

Remove the wrapper from the can of condensed milk.

Bring a small pot of water to a boil and carefully place the can in the water, making sure the can is completely submerged.

Boil for 1½ hours, adding water as necessary. Carefully remove the can from the water, turn it over, and return it to the water.

Return to a boil, and boil for an additional 1½ hours. I like to do three to four cans at a time, because it is such a lengthy process.

Remove the can from the water and let it cool to room temperature. Open the can and scoop the dulce de leche into an airtight container. Use as desired and store in the refrigerator.

BUTTER GANACHE

YIELD: 3 CUPS / **ACTIVE TIME:** 10 MINUTES / **TOTAL TIME:** 10 MINUTES

INGREDIENTS

2 cups dark chocolate

1 cup butter

Fill a medium saucepan halfway with water and bring to a simmer. Place the chocolate and butter in a bain-marie or heatproof bowl, place it over the simmering water, and stir until the mixture has emulsified. Remove the container from heat and let the ganache cool to room temperature before using as desired.

PASTRY CREAM

YIELD: 2 CUPS / **ACTIVE TIME:** 20 MINUTES / **TOTAL TIME:** 30 MINUTES

INGREDIENTS

1½ cups plus ⅓ cup whole milk

½ cup sugar

⅓ cup cornstarch

3 eggs

1½ teaspoons vanilla paste

2 tablespoons unsalted butter

Pinch of kosher salt

Place 1½ cups of milk and ¼ cup of sugar in a medium saucepan and warm over medium heat, whisking to dissolve the sugar and making sure that the mixture does not come to a boil.

Place the remaining milk and the cornstarch in a bowl and whisk to combine.

In a separate small bowl, whisk the eggs and remaining sugar together. Add the mixture to the cornstarch slurry.

While whisking continually, add one-quarter of the hot mixture to the egg mixture. Add the tempered egg mixture to the saucepan and cook over medium heat, whisking continually and scraping the bottom of the pan occasionally, until the custard has thickened, 6 to 8 minutes.

Remove the pan from heat and stir in the vanilla, butter, and salt. Place plastic wrap directly on the surface of the pastry cream to prevent a skin from forming and let it cool to room temperature. Use as desired.

CHANTILLY

YIELD: 2 CUPS / **ACTIVE TIME:** 20 MINUTES / **TOTAL TIME:** 20 MINUTES

INGREDIENTS

1½ cups heavy cream

1 teaspoon vanilla paste

2 tablespoons confectioners' sugar

Place all of the ingredients in the work bowl of a stand mixer fitted with the whisk attachment and whip until the mixture holds medium peaks. Use immediately.

MACERATED STRAWBERRIES

YIELD: 4 CUPS / **ACTIVE TIME:** 5 MINUTES / **TOTAL TIME:** 1 HOUR

INGREDIENTS

4 cups strawberries, hulled and sliced

½ cup sugar

1 teaspoon vanilla paste

2 tablespoons orange juice

Place all of the ingredients in a bowl and toss to combine.

Cover the bowl with plastic wrap and let the strawberries macerate in a naturally warm spot for at least 1 hour. Use as desired.

GRAHAM CRACKER CRUMB

YIELD: 8 CUPS / **ACTIVE TIME:** 10 MINUTES / **TOTAL TIME:** 1 HOUR

INGREDIENTS

½ cup brown sugar

½ cup sugar

½ cup honey

1 lb. unsalted butter, softened

5 cups all-purpose flour

1 tablespoon kosher salt

1 tablespoon baking soda

1 tablespoon cinnamon

Preheat the oven to 325°F on convection mode or 350°F for a conventional oven. Line a baking sheet with a Silpat mat.

Place the brown sugar, sugar, honey, and butter in the work bowl of a stand mixer fitted with the paddle attachment and beat until the mixture is light and fluffy, about 5 minutes. Add the remaining ingredients and beat until just incorporated.

Spread the mixture over the Silpat mat, place it in the oven, and bake until it is golden brown, about 20 minutes.

Remove the crumb mixture from the oven and let it cool to room temperature.

Place the crumb mixture in a food processor and pulse until it is fine crumbs. Use as desired.

MERINGUE

YIELD: 4 CUPS / ACTIVE TIME: 20 MINUTES / TOTAL TIME: 20 MINUTES

INGREDIENTS

2 cups sugar

1 cup egg whites

Place the sugar in a small saucepan and cook over medium heat until it is 240°F.

Place the egg whites in the work bowl of a stand mixer fitted with the whisk attachment and whip them on medium heat. Stream the hot sugar into the work bowl.

Raise the speed to high and whip until the meringue is cool, white, and glossy. Use immediately.

SOUR CREAM GLAZE

YIELD: 1 CUP / ACTIVE TIME: 10 MINUTES / TOTAL TIME: 10 MINUTES

INGREDIENTS

¼ cup sour cream

½ cup confectioners' sugar

½ teaspoon vanilla paste

Milk or water, as needed

Place the sour cream, confectioners' sugar, and vanilla paste in a bowl and whisk until the mixture just has a fluid consistency.

If the glaze seems too thick, incorporate a splash of milk or water. Use as desired.

WHITE CHOCOLATE GANACHE

YIELD: 2½ CUPS / ACTIVE TIME: 20 MINUTES / TOTAL TIME: 20 MINUTES

INGREDIENTS

2¼ cups white chocolate

¼ cup heavy cream

1 tablespoon glucose

⅓ cup unsalted butter, softened

Fill a medium saucepan halfway with water and bring to a simmer. Place the white chocolate in a bain-marie or heatproof bowl, place it over the simmering water, and stir until it is 90°F. Remove the container from heat and set the chocolate aside.

Place the heavy cream and glucose in a small saucepan and bring to a boil.

Pour the cream mixture over the white chocolate and stir until the mixture has emulsified. Add the butter and stir to incorporate. Let the ganache cool just enough that it won't melt a buttercream but can still be piped into cupcakes and use as desired.

STRAWBERRY RHUBARB COMPOTE

YIELD: 1½ CUPS / ACTIVE TIME: 10 MINUTES / TOTAL TIME: 10 MINUTES

INGREDIENTS

1¼ cups finely diced strawberries

Zest and juice of ½ lemon

½ cup sugar

1¼ cups finely diced rhubarb

3 tablespoons water

Place the strawberries, lemon zest, lemon juice, and half of the sugar in a small saucepan and warm over low heat until the sugar has melted and the strawberries start to release their juices, about 2 minutes. Remove the pan from heat, strain the juices into a bowl, and place the berries in a separate bowl.

Place the rhubarb, water, and remaining sugar in the saucepan and warm over low heat until the sugar has melted and rhubarb is tender, 4 to 5 minutes. Strain the rhubarb juices into the strawberry juices, pressing down on the rhubarb to extract as much liquid as possible. Add the rhubarb to the strawberries.

Place the juice mixture in the saucepan and cook over medium heat until it has reduced by half, making sure it does not burn.

Transfer the reduced juice to a bowl and stir in the strawberry-and-rhubarb mixture. Let the compote cool completely and then use as desired.

OAT CRUMBLE

INGREDIENTS

½ cup brown sugar

Pinch of kosher salt

1 cup oats

6 tablespoons
unsalted butter

YIELD: 1¾ CUPS / **ACTIVE TIME:** 10 MINUTES / **TOTAL TIME:** 50 MINUTES

Preheat the oven to 325°F on convection mode or 350°F for a conventional oven. Line a baking sheet with parchment paper and coat it with nonstick cooking spray.

Place the brown sugar, salt, and oats in a bowl and toss to combine.

Place the butter in a small saucepan and bring it to a boil. Stir in the oat mixture and then spread it on the baking sheet. Place in the oven and bake for 10 minutes.

Remove the pan from the oven and toss the crumble. Return it to the oven and bake until it is crispy and golden brown, 6 to 8 minutes, making sure that the oats don't burn.

Remove the crumble from the oven and let it cool to room temperature. Use as desired.

CANDIED PISTACHIOS

INGREDIENTS

Sugar, to taste

1 egg white

1 cup raw pistachios

YIELD: 1 CUP / **ACTIVE TIME:** 10 MINUTES / **TOTAL TIME:** 1 HOUR

Line a baking sheet with parchment paper. Add sugar to a shallow bowl.

Using a gloved hand, dip your fingers into the egg white and then gently rub the pistachios until they are coated. We are looking for the nuts to be fully coated without having any egg white dripping off.

Add the pistachios to the sugar and toss until they are delicately coated. Place the pistachios on the baking sheet and place it in a naturally warm spot. Let the sugar harden around the pistachios for 1 to 3 hours. If your home seems too cool for the pistachios to become candied in this manner, simply preheat your oven to 200°F and then turn it off. Place the pistachios in the oven for about 1 hour.

BOURBON PEACH COMPOTE

INGREDIENTS

2 ripe, firm peaches,
peeled and finely diced

¼ cup sugar

2 tablespoons bourbon

1 teaspoon vanilla paste

YIELD: 2 CUPS / **ACTIVE TIME:** 15 MINUTES / **TOTAL TIME:** 15 MINUTES

Place the peaches and sugar in a medium saucepan and warm over low heat, stirring continually, until the sugar starts to caramelize. Deglaze the pan with the bourbon and stir until the sugar has dissolved, about 30 seconds.

Remove the pan from heat and stir in the vanilla paste. Let the compote cool to room temperature and use as desired.

SUGARED BERRIES

INGREDIENTS

Sugar, to taste

Assorted berries,
to taste

1 egg white

YIELD: 1 SERVING / **ACTIVE TIME:** 15 MINUTES / **TOTAL TIME:** 15 MINUTES

Line a baking sheet with parchment paper. Place sugar in a shallow bowl. Rinse the berries well and pat them dry. Place the egg white in a bowl and whisk until it is frothy.

Dip the berries into the egg white and then toss them in the sugar. Place them on the baking sheet and let them sit at room temperature until the sugar hardens into a shell. Use as desired.

MANGO GANACHE

INGREDIENTS

½ cup mango puree

2⅔ cups white chocolate

¼ cup heavy cream

2 tablespoons glucose

1⅓ tablespoons unsalted butter, softened

YIELD: 1 CUP / **ACTIVE TIME:** 10 MINUTES / **TOTAL TIME:** 10 MINUTES

Place the mango puree in a saucepan and warm it over medium heat until it has reduced by half. Place the white chocolate in a heatproof bowl and pour the reduced mango puree over it.

Place the heavy cream and glucose in a small saucepan and bring to a boil.

Pour the cream mixture into the white chocolate mixture. Let the mixture sit for 30 seconds and then stir until it is smooth. Add the butter and stir to incorporate. Let the ganache cool just enough that it won't melt a buttercream but can still be piped into cupcakes and use as desired.

APRICOT JAM

INGREDIENTS

4 cups apricots, peeled and pitted

3 cups sugar

2 tablespoons fresh lemon juice

½ teaspoon unsalted butter

1 teaspoon vanilla paste

YIELD: 4 CUPS / **ACTIVE TIME:** 45 MINUTES / **TOTAL TIME:** 45 MINUTES

Place the apricots, sugar, lemon juice, and butter in a large saucepan and bring to a boil. Cook until the mixture thickens, about 25 minutes, stirring frequently.

Remove the pan from heat and skim off any foam. Stir in the vanilla, place plastic wrap directly on the surface of the jam, and let it cool to room temperature. Use as desired.

APPLE CHIPS

INGREDIENTS

2 apples

Confectioners' sugar, to taste

YIELD: 18 CHIPS / **ACTIVE TIME:** 20 MINUTES

TOTAL TIME: 3 HOURS AND 20 MINUTES

Preheat the oven to 175°F on convection mode or 200°F for a conventional oven. Use a dehydrator if you have one and are familiar with it.

Line a baking sheet with a Silpat mat. Using a mandoline or a sharp knife, cut the apples as thin as possible and place them on the baking sheet. Generously dust the apples with confectioners' sugar and place them in the oven. Dehydrate them for 2 hours.

Remove the apples from the oven, turn them over, and generously dust them with more confectioners' sugar. Return the apples to the oven and dehydrate them until they are light and crispy, about 1 hour.

Remove the apple chips from the oven and let them cool. Use as desired.

WHIPPED CREAM

INGREDIENTS

2 cups heavy cream

1 tablespoon vanilla paste

YIELD: 2 CUPS / **ACTIVE TIME:** 10 MINUTES / **TOTAL TIME:** 10 MINUTES

Place the heavy cream and vanilla in the work bowl of a stand mixer fitted with the whisk attachment and whip until the mixture holds stiff peaks. Use as desired.

CARAMEL CORN

YIELD: 1½ CUPS / **ACTIVE TIME:** 20 MINUTES
TOTAL TIME: 1 HOUR AND 30 MINUTES

INGREDIENTS

½ cup dried corn kernels

1 tablespoon canola oil

½ cup brown sugar

⅓ cup corn syrup

⅓ cup unsalted butter

½ teaspoon baking soda

Sea salt, to taste

Preheat the oven to 225°F on convection mode or 250°F for a conventional oven. Line a baking sheet with a Silpat mat.

Place the corn and canola oil in a large pot and warm over medium heat, gently shaking the pot until the corn starts to pop. Place a sheet pan over the pot, hold it in place with one hand, and continue to shake the pot until all of the corn has popped.

Coat a large metal bowl with nonstick cooking spray and place the popcorn in it. Set the popcorn aside.

Place the brown sugar, corn syrup, and butter in a small saucepan and bring to a boil, stirring until the caramel is smooth. Carefully stir in the baking soda, pour the caramel over the popcorn, and toss to coat. Quickly transfer the caramel corn to the baking sheet, season it with salt, and place it in the oven.

Bake until the caramel has hardened, about 1 hour, tossing the caramel corn every 15 minutes. Remove the caramel corn from the oven and let it cool. Separate the clusters and use as desired.

CANDIED CRANBERRIES

YIELD: 1 CUP / **ACTIVE TIME:** 15 MINUTES
TOTAL TIME: 2 HOURS AND 15 MINUTES

INGREDIENTS

½ cup sugar, plus more to taste

¼ cup water

1 cup cranberries

Line a baking sheet with parchment paper.

Place the sugar and water in a small saucepan and bring to a boil, stirring to dissolve the sugar. Cook until the syrup starts to thicken, 3 to 4 minutes. Add the cranberries, reduce the heat, and stir to coat. Too much heat and agitation will pop the cranberries, so we want to work quickly but gently when coating the cranberries. The syrup should stick on the outside of the cranberries, not drip off.

Strain the cranberries. Add sugar to a shallow bowl, add the cranberries, and toss to coat. Place the cranberries on the baking sheet, place them in a naturally warm spot and let the syrup harden for 2 hours.

APPLE BUTTER

YIELD: 4 CUPS / **ACTIVE TIME:** 20 MINUTES / **TOTAL TIME:** 40 MINUTES

INGREDIENTS

8 apples, chopped

1 cup apple cider

1 cup sugar

½ cup brown sugar

½ cup lemon juice

¼ cup apple cider vinegar

2 tablespoons vanilla paste

Pinch of kosher salt

1 tablespoon Spice Girl Mix (see page 254)

Water, as needed

Preheat the oven to 325°F on convection mode or 350°F for a conventional oven. Place the apples, cider, sugar, brown sugar, lemon juice, and vinegar in a Dutch oven and place it in the oven. Bake until the apples are tender and the sugars have caramelized, about 1 hour.

Remove the pot from the oven and transfer the mixture to a blender. Add the vanilla, salt, and spice mix and puree until smooth. If the apple butter is too thick for your liking, stream in a bit of water to thin it out. Let the apple butter cool and use as desired.

WHITE CHOCOLATE MOCHA GANACHE

YIELD: ½ CUP / **ACTIVE TIME:** 15 MINUTES / **TOTAL TIME:** 45 MINUTES

INGREDIENTS

1¾ cups white chocolate

⅓ cup heavy cream

2 tablespoons glucose

1 tablespoon unsalted butter, softened

2 teaspoons Trablit Coffee Extract

Fill a medium saucepan halfway with water and bring to a simmer. Place the white chocolate in a bain-marie or heatproof bowl, place it over the simmering water, and stir until it is smooth. Remove the container from heat and let the white chocolate cool to 90°F.

Place the heavy cream and glucose in a small saucepan and bring to a boil.

Pour the cream mixture over the white chocolate and let the mixture sit for 30 seconds. Stir until it is smooth, add the butter and coffee extract, and stir to incorporate. Let the ganache cool just enough that it won't melt a buttercream but can still be piped into cupcakes and use as desired.

DEHYDRATED ORANGES

YIELD: 18 SLICES / **ACTIVE TIME:** 30 MINUTES / **TOTAL TIME:** 3 HOURS

INGREDIENTS

2 oranges

Preheat the oven to the lowest possible temperature. If you have a dehydrator, set it for 130°F.

Rinse the oranges well and cut them into ¼-inch-thick slices.

Arrange the orange slices on a parchment-lined baking sheet or a dehydrator tray, removing all of the seeds and making sure the slices to not overlap.

Let the oranges dry until they are completely dehydrated, 6 to 12 hours, rotating the pan or tray and turning the slices over occasionally. If using the oven, check on the oranges a little more often to make sure they do not burn.

Remove the dehydrated oranges from the oven, let them cool, and use as desired.

CANDIED HAZELNUTS

YIELD: 2 CUPS / **ACTIVE TIME:** 20 MINUTES / **TOTAL TIME:** 40 MINUTES

INGREDIENTS

4½ oz. sugar

1¾ oz. water

9 oz. raw hazelnuts

1 tablespoon unsalted butter

Pinch of flaky sea salt

1 teaspoon vanilla paste

Line a baking sheet with a Silpat mat. Place the sugar and water in a small saucepan and bring to a boil, stirring to dissolve the sugar. Add the hazelnuts and stir continually until the hazelnuts are completely coated and the sugar has caramelized, turning a beautiful amber.

Remove the pan from heat, add the butter, salt, and vanilla, and stir to combine. Immediately transfer the hazelnuts to the baking sheet. Add some water to the pan to prevent the sugar from burning.

Working with a couple of spoons or latex gloves on your hands, separate the hazelnuts from each other so they do not stick together. Let the hazelnuts cool for about 10 minutes and use as desired.

GINGERBREAD GANACHE

YIELD: 2 CUPS / **ACTIVE TIME:** 15 MINUTES / **TOTAL TIME:** 30 MINUTES

INGREDIENTS

10 tablespoons unsalted butter, softened

1 teaspoon Spice Girl Mix (see page 254)

½ cup molasses

14 oz. milk chocolate, melted

1¾ oz. Pernod

Place the butter, spice mix, and molasses in a bowl and stir until thoroughly combined. Slowly stream in the melted chocolate, carefully folding the mixture to prevent lumps from forming.

Add the Pernod and stir to combine. Cover the ganache with plastic wrap and let it sit at room temperature until it reaches a pipable consistency, about 15 minutes. Use as desired.

SPIKED EGGNOG GANACHE

YIELD: 2 CUPS / **ACTIVE TIME:** 20 MINUTES / **TOTAL TIME:** 20 MINUTES

INGREDIENTS

- 1½ cups white chocolate
- ½ cup unsalted butter, softened
- 1 tablespoon glucose
- ½ teaspoon freshly grated nutmeg
- 1½ teaspoons vanilla paste
- 2 tablespoons dark rum

Fill a medium saucepan halfway with water and bring to a simmer. Place the white chocolate in a bain-marie or heatproof bowl, place it over the simmering water, and stir until it is smooth. Remove the container from heat and let the white chocolate cool to 90°F.

Place the butter, glucose, nutmeg, and vanilla in the work bowl of a stand mixer fitted with the paddle attachment and beat until the mixture is fluffy. With the mixer running, slowly stream in the white chocolate. Slowly stream in the rum and beat to incorporate. Let the ganache cool just enough that it won't melt a buttercream but can still be piped into cupcakes and use as desired.

PEANUT BRITTLE

YIELD: 10 SERVINGS / **ACTIVE TIME:** 10 MINUTES
TOTAL TIME: 40 MINUTES

INGREDIENTS

- 1 cup sugar
- ¼ cup water
- ¼ cup unsalted butter, softened
- ⅛ cup light corn syrup
- ¼ teaspoon baking soda
- 1 cup plus 2 teaspoons peanuts
- Flaky sea salt, to taste

Line a baking sheet with a Silpat mat. Place the sugar, water, butter, and corn syrup in a medium saucepan and bring to a boil over medium heat, carefully stirring with a wooden spoon. Cook until the caramel is 300°F.

Working quickly and carefully, remove the pan from heat and add the baking soda, which will cause the caramel to bubble. Stir for 5 to 10 seconds to incorporate and then immediately add the peanuts. Toss them in the caramel and quickly turn them out onto the baking sheet. Press down on the peanuts to spread them into an even layer and generously season with flaky sea salt.

Let the peanut brittle cool for at least 30 minutes before using as desired. Store in an airtight container at room temperature, as peanut brittle doesn't do well in the refrigerator.

CHOCOLATE SOIL

YIELD: 2 CUPS / **ACTIVE TIME:** 20 MINUTES / **TOTAL TIME:** 1 HOUR

INGREDIENTS

- 6½ tablespoons unsalted butter
- ⅓ cup cocoa powder
- ¾ cup all-purpose flour
- 7 tablespoons sugar
- ¼ teaspoon kosher salt

Preheat the oven to 325°F on convection mode or 350°F for a conventional oven. Line a baking sheet with parchment paper.

Place all of the ingredients in the work bowl of a stand mixer fitted with the paddle attachment and beat until the mixture comes together as a loose, crumbly dough, 3 to 5 minutes. Place the mixture on the baking sheet, place it in the oven, and bake for 20 minutes.

Remove the mixture from the oven and let it cool for 20 minutes.

Place the mixture in a food processor and pulse until it is fine crumbs. Use as desired.

Conversion Table

WEIGHTS

1 oz. = 28 grams

2 oz. = 57 grams

4 oz. (¼ lb.) = 113 grams

8 oz. (½ lb.) = 227 grams

16 oz. (1 lb.) = 454 grams

VOLUME MEASURES

⅛ teaspoon = 0.6 ml

¼ teaspoon = 1.23 ml

½ teaspoon = 2.5 ml

1 teaspoon = 5 ml

1 tablespoon (3 teaspoons) = ½ fluid oz. = 15 ml

2 tablespoons = 1 fluid oz. = 29.5 ml

¼ cup (4 tablespoons) = 2 fluid oz. = 59 ml

⅓ cup (5⅓ tablespoons) = 2.7 fluid oz. = 80 ml

½ cup (8 tablespoons) = 4 fluid oz. = 120 ml

⅔ cup (10⅔ tablespoons) = 5.4 fluid oz. = 160 ml

¾ cup (12 tablespoons) = 6 fluid oz. = 180 ml

1 cup (16 tablespoons) = 8 fluid oz. = 240 ml

TEMPERATURE EQUIVALENTS

°F	°C	Gas Mark
225	110	¼
250	130	½
275	140	1
300	150	2
325	170	3
350	180	4
375	190	5
400	200	6
425	220	7
450	230	8
475	240	9
500	250	10

LENGTH MEASURES

¹⁄₁₆ inch = 1.6 mm

⅛ inch = 3 mm

¼ inch = 6.35 mm

½ inch = 1.25 cm

¾ inch = 2 cm

1 inch = 2.5 cm

Index

About the Author

GABRIELLE (GABBY) COTE is the sole proprietor and cake designer behind Big Fish Cake Studio, a bespoke cake shop in Southern Maine. She graduated from The Culinary Institute of America with a degree in Baking & Pastry Arts in 2011. She then made her way to Southern Maine, where she began working as a bakery assistant at the prestigious White Barn Inn in Kennebunkport. After years of working through the bakery and pastry departments and becoming the Executive Pastry Chef, she found herself cooking savory as well, and spent her last few years at the White Barn Inn as Sous Chef. She left the White Barn Inn in 2017 and went across town to Earth at Hidden Pond, where she was Sous Chef for three seasons. Eager to get out of professional kitchens, in early 2020 Gabby and her partner Derek began to build their dream studio, featuring a commercial kitchen, client meeting room, and spacious photo studio. She then started Big Fish Cake Studio, believing that a return to her pastry roots would be best. Since opening Big Fish, Gabby has helped thousands of locals celebrate and make memories. She has been voted year after year as "Best Of" by The Knot for Southern Maine wedding vendors, and has been featured on News Center Maine's *Maine Life* and in the magazines in *edible Maine* and *Real Maine Weddings*.

PRAISE FOR
Let Them Eat Cupcakes

With her first cookbook, Chef Gabby Cote ushers us into her kitchen—a clean, cozy, brick-lined space where we can sit down with a freshly brewed cappuccino and learn a very particular kind of magic. Gabby's lessons are friendly, encouraging, and best of all—FUN! They cover everything from the easiest way to keep your workspace clean and inspiring and foundational recipes that serve as foolproof baker's building blocks to a cupcake recipe for literally EVERY occasion. Gabby somehow manages to both astutely demystify cupcake creation and still maintain a childlike sense of whimsy with every recipe and mouthwatering photo—a tone that is just as right for beginners as it is for lifelong bakers who are willing to risk falling in love with their craft all over again.

—KATE SHAFFER, Owner/Founder of Ragged Coast Chocolates, cookbook author, and home baker

Wow what a fabulous and scrumptious cookbook. The pages ahead share beautiful cupcake recipes that Gabby has mastered over many years of experimenting. I am so glad I have Gabby as a friend and my go-to person for all of the moments in life where something sweet makes it even sweeter. One of the most talented pastry chefs I have had the pleasure of working alongside. Her flavor combinations, artistic presentation, and eye for detail are all present in this magnificent book. Gabby is a talented and accomplished Pastry Chef with a true passion for creating cakes, and this shines through in this book. I, along with all home cooks, look forward to making these remarkable creations from Gabby's elegant book for the next momentous occasion—or any occasion, because life is more beautiful after you eat a cupcake.

—JONATHAN CARTWRIGHT, Chef/Owner

About Cider Mill Press Book Publishers

Good ideas ripen with time. From seed to harvest, Cider Mill Press brings fine reading, information, and entertainment together between the covers of its creatively crafted books. Our Cider Mill bears fruit twice a year, publishing a new crop of titles each spring and fall.

"Where Good Books Are Ready for Press"
501 Nelson Place
Nashville, Tennessee 37214

cidermillpress.com